Men as Workers in
Services for Young Children:
Issues of a Mixed Gender Workforce

Thomas Coram Research Unit
Institute of Education, University of London

Men as Workers in Services for Young Children: Issues of a Mixed Gender Workforce

Proceedings of a seminar
held at Henley on Thames, 29–31 May 1997

Edited by
Charlie Owen, Claire Cameron and Peter Moss

Bedford Way Papers

INSTITUTE OF
EDUCATION
UNIVERSITY OF LONDON

First published in 1998 by the Institute of Education University of London,
20 Bedford Way, London WC1H 0AL

Pursuing Excellence in Education

British Library Cataloguing in Publication Data;
a catalogue record for this publication is available from the British Library

ISBN 0 85473 533X

Design by Joan Rose
Page make-up by Cambridge Photosetting, Cambridge

Production services by
Book Production Consultants plc, Cambridge

Printed by Formara Ltd, Southend on Sea, Essex

October 1998

List of Contributors

Leif Ærø
Viborg-Seminariet, Denmark

Andy Bateman
Sheffield Children's Centre

Claire Cameron
Thomas Coram Research Unit, Institute of Education, University of London

Trevor Chandler
Pen Green Centre

Björn Flising
University of Gothenburg, Department of Education

Erik Hauglund
Royal Ministry of Children and Family Affairs, Oslo, Norway

Jytte Juul Jensen
Jydsk Paedagog-Seminarium, Risskov, Denmark

Susan J. Kelley
College of Health and Human Sciences, Georgia State University, Atlanta, GA

Johanna Lammi-Taskula
Stakes (National Research and Development Centre for Welfare and Health), Helsinki, Finland

Charlie Lewis
Lancaster University, UK

Lars Maanum
Hauketo Barnehage, Oslo, Norway

Chrissy Meleady
Sheffield Children's Centre

Peter Moss
Thomas Coram Research Unit.

Tommie Nilsen
Hauketo Barnehage, Oslo, Norway

Charlie Owen
Thomas Coram Research Unit, Institute of Education, University of London

Helen Penn
Social Science Research Unit, Institute of Education, University of London

Sandy Pepperell
Roehampton Institute, London

Keith Pringle
University of Sunderland

Sarah Robinson
Nursing Research Unit, King's College, London University

Svein Ole Satagen
Sogn and Fjordane College, Sogndal, Norway

Sue Smedley
Roehampton Institute, London

Kenny Spence
Greendykes Children's Centre, Edinburgh

Erna Sundqvist
Gothenburg, Sweden

Jari-Matti Vuorio
University of Helsinki, Finland

Jo Warin
Lancaster University, UK

Robin Wright
Bournemouth and Poole College of Further Education

Contents

Part 4 Risks, Allegations and Protection: Does Having More Male Workers Increase the Risks for Young Children and What Can Be Done to Protect Children from Risk and Workers from False Allegations?

Part 5 Training and Recruiting Men to Work in Services for Young Children: Are there Effective Strategies for Developing a Mixed-gender Workforce?

Part 6 Conclusions

PART 1

Introduction

1 Men as Workers in Services for Young Children: Prolegomena

Charlie Owen

Thomas Coram Research Unit, Institute of Education, University of London

Introduction

The employment of men in the care of young children is a topic which generates much excitement. On the one hand there are those who argue that the patriarchal organization of society, sexual inequality and male violence will never be changed whilst men are allowed to opt out of the most human of activities: caring for children. On the other hand, there are those who think that men are so dangerous – physically, but especially sexually – that they should not be allowed to take part in such a crucially sensitive activity as caring for children, especially when the effects of sexual abuse can persist for generations.

Most of us probably share some elements of each of these two caricatured viewpoints. We are pulled in one direction or another by events: another report of genocide or ethnic cleansing makes us think that if only men could be raised as more caring these things would not happen; then another press report about paedophiles shocks us with how disgusting men can be and we are made suspicious of even apparently nice men. However, whilst we grapple with these anxieties there are men quietly getting on with their jobs of caring for children: should we be pleased or worried? Should we be encouraging more men into childcare or should we be raising barriers against them? To coin a phrase, what is to be done?

To discuss these important issues, and to see what is already being done, three members of the Thomas Coram Research Unit, of the Institute of Education, University of London – Charlie Owen, Peter Moss and Claire Cameron – convened an international seminar with the title

'Men as Workers in Services for Young Children: Issues of a Mixed-gender Workforce'. Attendance was by invitation. This created its own problems in that there were too many people to invite. The limited places could have been filled several times over, and many people who could have contributed were unfortunately not there. Participants included researchers, policy-makers, childcare workers and those involved in training. They came mostly from Great Britain; one came from the United States; and importantly – for reasons that will become clear later – there were a number of participants from the Nordic countries of Denmark, Finland, Norway and Sweden.

However, before embarking on the proceedings themselves, I would like to make a few preliminary remarks, by way of contextualizing the discussion. This is not an introduction, as Claire Cameron and Peter Moss together provide an introduction to both the seminar and these proceedings. These remarks are more of a prologue, written with the benefit of hindsight.

Consensus

I think it is fair to say that there was a fair degree of consensus in the meeting that we wanted more men to be working in the care of young children. However, there was less agreement as to *why* there should be more men. The sorts of reasons put forward were of two kinds: either individual ones or those of social equality.

The individual reasons included the benefits to individual children – both boys and girls – such as the benefit of absorbing male role models of caring and of men more generally. Opportunities for rough and tumble play came up several times, again both for boys and girls: the Scandinavians, in particular, thought this was more likely with male staff. There were thought to be individual benefits not just for the children, but for the male workers, the female workers and for the parents.

Social equality reasons were more to do with gender in the workforce, both in general and specifically in the area of childcare. Childcare is an occupation where traditionally relatively few men have worked, so men working in childcare is in itself a challenge to the sexual division of labour. In particular, men as childcare workers were seen to be entering the most archetypal female occupation, thus eroding distinctions of masculine and feminine. To have more men working as carers of young children was also seen as a way of challenging the gendered nature of violence, counterposing care (female) with aggression (male).

To me it seems crucial that if some jobs are designated as exclusively for women, then there will be no shortage of people wanting to argue that there must be some jobs for which only men are suitable. It also seems likely that these might be jobs such as running industry or the government. Any argument for a sexual division of labour that relies on the essential natures of men and women leaves open the possibility of arguing that sexual inequalities are immutable. If the argument instead relies on differences between men and women that have arisen due to socialization, then there must be some point at which the circle of social reproduction of differences can be broken, and the employment of men in childcare might just be that point.

What a difference a man makes

It was reported at the seminar (by Charlie Lewis) that psychological research has shown no consistent individual differences between those who receive different levels of care from their fathers. Some people might take this as an argument against the need to employ more men in childcare: if children are not affected by the amount of time they spend with their fathers, then perhaps the amount of time they spend with male childcare workers is equally irrelevant. However, this must surely be good news, because it means that children growing up without a father present (e.g. with lone mothers or lesbian mothers) are not deprived of some vital ingredient that only men can give. However, no-one would use this as an argument for excluding fathers from contact with their own children, and passing childcare back to the exclusive concern of mothers. No more should it be used as an argument for expecting women to be the exclusive employed childcarers.

Moreover, a different psychological perspective, from psychoanalysis, has suggested that it is exclusive early female care itself which reproduces patterns of masculinity and femininity, and the dominance of male over female:

> *women remain almost universally in charge of infant and early child-care. What is important is the effect of predominantly female care on the later emotional predilections of the child*: The point of crucial consequences is *that for virtually every living person it is a woman – usually the mother – who has provided the main initial contact with humanity and with nature.* (Dinnerstein, 1976: 26, emphasis as original)

> The sexual division of labour and women's responsibility for childcare are linked to and generate male dominance. Psychologists have demonstrated unequivocally that the very fact of being mothered by a woman generates in men conflicts over masculinity, a psychology of male dominance, and a need to be superior to women. ... Thus the social organization of parenting produces sexual inequality, not simply role differentiation.   (Chodorow, 1978: 214)

This is a contentious view, as Charlie Lewis makes clear in Chapter 8. However, even some of those who accept the significance of early mothering still stress that the involvement of men in childcare is only one of the things that needs to be changed to achieve greater gender equality. As Lynne Segal puts it:

> Chodorow in the US, Eichenbaum and Orbach in Britain, and most of the other writers in this field argue passionately that the way to create gender equality directly, and a better world contingently, is to involve men as well as women in the care of young children. I would agree that this is an important strategy for gender equality. ... However, I think their emphasis on the psychological underestimates the obstacles in the way of such a strategy, and exaggerates the extent to which it could, on its own, either overturn conventional gender relations or transform 'the sorry state of things entire'.   (Segal, 1987: 156)
>   Masculinity, like femininity, is systematically produced throughout a whole lifetime, and for boys connects with the physical strength built up through competitive sport, the skills acquired through education and

the use of tools and other technology, the ideologies of sexual performance, the segregation of the workforce, the experience of family
life, and the inescapable weight of cultural image and definitions that
ubiquitously enclose us. (Segal, 1987: 152)

Abuse

The seminar spent quite some time on the issues of abuse and the
potential dangers of men to children. This included periods of mutual
incomprehension: the Scandinavians seemed truly baffled by what they
saw as the British and US obsession with sexual abuse. They seemed to
be convinced that this was part of an Anglo-Saxon prurient preoccupation
with other people's sexual behaviour. At one point, a British story was
being told of a father, separated from his child's mother, who had related
that he felt unable to have any physical contact with his preschool
daughter in case it was interpreted as abuse and he was consequently
denied access to her. Unable to contain themselves any longer, some
started to shout out, 'That's abuse! *That's* abuse!'

It would be easy to characterize the Scandinavians as complacent in
their ignorance, just waiting for a scandal to break – as the terrible
paedophile murders in Belgium did just before the conference. As
Chapter 11 makes clear, the Nordic countries are not immune to these
cases, nor are they indifferent to them. However, they are not willing to
let the potential danger of abuse dominate all other considerations, in
particular the rights of children to have the experience of both male and
female carers.

There was some dispute over the extent of abuse in day care, and some
acceptance that it may vary between countries. On the other hand, it was
pointed out that absence of evidence does not amount to evidence of
absence and most abuse may be unrevealed. It was a salutary reminder
that not so long ago we did not know about sexual abuse in residential
children's homes, nor in their own homes. It was only investigations
following a few initial revelations that brought to light the extent of these
abuses – the full extent of which we may still not have uncovered.

A point that was made forcefully by a number of participants was that, although abuse is predominantly carried out by men, it is not exclusively so. The most extensive research on abuse in day nurseries, conducted by Finkelhor, Williams and Burns (1988) in the United States, found that 40 per cent of abusers in day nurseries were women. Of course, the other 60 per cent came from the tiny minority of men who worked in the nurseries or from other men. Only two-thirds of the male abusers were nursery workers – either childcare workers or peripheral workers, such as bus drivers or cleaners – the rest were predominantly young male relatives of 'family day carers', or what in Britain would be called childminders. From these data, it is clear that eliminating male day care workers will not eliminate the abuse. We need procedures to protect children, and not just from men.

Gender pedagogy

Another thing the Scandinavians brought to the seminar was the concept of gender pedagogy. This is the idea that girls and boys behave in different ways, and that this must be taken account of in the organization of childcare if the needs of both girls and boys are to be met. This idea of gender pedagogy is a reaction to the theory and practice that all be-havioural differences between girls and boys are socially conditioned and that, in the interests of developing balanced adults, all children should be treated the same. Instead, gender pedagogy says that girls and boys – to some extent – have different needs, so that to treat them the same is to do them a disservice. Further than that, gender pedagogy says that women and men care in different ways, and that these too need to be accom-modated within day care: not just women for the girls and men for the boys, but that both girls and boys should experience the different ways of women and men as a normal part of their development.

What sort of differences are we are talking about – that boys more often choose more active, noisy games, including more play fighting; that men are more tolerant of 'dangerous' play; and so on? These may sound suspiciously like gender stereotypes, and the question was raised as to the extent to which a gender pedagogy is merely adapting to gender stereotypes rather than catering for gender differences. Recent work on masculinity tends to emphasize the diversity of masculinities rather than trying to identify what is essentially masculine (e.g. Connell, 1995). However, the gender pedagogy model, as explained during the seminar, does not aim to push girls or boys into particular ways of behaving defined as feminine or masculine, but instead demands respect for difference. The dominant, 'gender neutral' pedagogy which aims to treat everyone the same, was argued not to respect differences but to try to suppress them. The same arguments would apply to female and male staff. They must be able to be different from each other, but also not to be pushed into gender stereotyped directions: it is not for women to bandage knees and mop the floor while the men play rough games and change the light bulbs.

How to get more men into childcare

The seminar spent quite a lot of time on the subject of how to get more men into childcare. Many useful strategies were suggested. However, two issues came up again and again: these were pay-and-conditions and status. It was generally agreed that for more men to enter the profession there would have to be an increase in the poor pay received by childcare workers and improvements in their conditions of employment. Linked with those changes was the need to raise the status of childcare as an occupation. Although it was agreed that these were useful aims not just in order to recruit more men but for childcare workers anyway, it was seen as a little insulting to the women who have had to tolerate these conditions up to now that a spotlight is only turned onto their pay, conditions and status when it is a question of attracting more men.

We heard of successful examples of strategies from the Nordic countries to increase the number of male students on childcare courses, to recruit more male workers and to retain them in post, without them being promoted out of contact with the children. A clear message from the examples was that, to be successful, someone needs to take responsibility. In Norway it was the state; in Sweden, the local authority and the colleges. A strong message from the seminar was that it is time for someone to take responsibility in the UK.

The seminar

Those who took part in this seminar will have a number of shared memories, in addition to those listed in the proceedings themselves. The seminar took place over two gloriously hot days in May, 1997, in the beautiful setting of the sixteenth-century Red Lion Hotel in Henley on Thames. We were well looked after by the staff there. Most of the meeting took place in two adjacent rooms, one for the conference and the other for meals. However, there were not enough gilded chairs to furnish both rooms, so we all had to carry our chairs with us between rooms. In addition to the staff of the Red Lion, there are many people who deserve thanks, but we want particularly to thank Caroline Bell (the project administrator), Steve Martin (the conference organizer) and the Department of Health. The latter supported the seminar financially, for which we are very grateful, although – of course – nothing said at the seminar and nothing written here can be taken to be the views of the Department of Health. What you have here are the proceedings of the seminar. I hope you will judge them to be as worthwhile as we found the seminar itself.

References

Chodorow, N. (1978), *The Reproduction of Mothering*. Berkeley: University of California Press.

Connell, R.W. (1995), *Masculinities*. Cambridge: Polity Press.

Dinnerstein, D. (1976), *The Rocking of the Cradle and the Ruling of the World*. London: Souvenir Press.

Finkelhor, D., Williams, L.M. and Burns, N. (1988), *Nursery Crimes: Sexual Abuse in Day care*. Newbury Park, CA: Sage.

Segal, L. (1987), *Is the Future Female?* London: Virago.

2 Men as Carers for Children: An Introduction

Claire Cameron and Peter Moss
Thomas Coram Research Unit, Institute of Education, University of London

A European issue

This seminar has its origins in two places – Brussels and London. Back in 1986, the European Commission established an expert network to provide support to the Commission's Equal Opportunities Unit on the broad subject of reconciling employment with the care and upbringing of children. Peter Moss was asked to coordinate this Childcare Network, working with colleagues from each of the then 12 member states. The work of the Network – renamed the European Commission Network on Childcare and Other Measures to Reconcile Employment and Family Responsibilities of Women and Men – originally focused on services providing care for children. Over time, however, the focus broadened to include other issues, in particular leave arrangements – such as parental and paternity leave – and measures to support more equal sharing of caring responsibilities between women and men (for a report of the Network's activities and a full list of publications, see EC Childcare Network, 1996).

In March 1992, the Council of Ministers – that is the member state governments – adopted a Council Recommendation on Childcare (92/241/EEC). Unlike a Directive, a Recommendation is not legally binding, but it is an important political statement, expressing principles and objectives agreed by all member states. The Recommendation's objective was 'to encourage initiatives to enable women and men to reconcile employment with the care and upbringing of children' (Article 1). These initiatives were grouped under four headings. The first three e services (Article 3), leave arrangements for employed parents (Article 4), and the environment, structure and organization of the workplace (Article 5). The fourth area concerned the sharing of responsibilities between women and men. Article 6 of the Recommendation states:

> As regards responsibilities arising from the care and upbringing of children, it is recommended that member states should promote and encourage, with due respect for freedom of the individual, increased participation by men, in order to achieve a more equal sharing of parental responsibilities between men and women and to enable women to have a more effective role in the labour market.

This recommendation for action, however, is not an isolated example. It is one of a series of similar statements, going back to at least the early 1980s, in which the various institutions of the EU – the Commission, the Parliament, the Council of Ministers – have called for change in the gendered nature of childcare, involving men assuming more responsibility. For example, in the *European Social Policy: Options for the Union (Green Paper)* the European Commission (1993) refers to:

> the gender-based division of family and employment responsibilities not only constraining women's lives but also depriving men of the emotional rewards resulting from the care and development of children.

In its 1994 White Paper on Social Policy, the Commission again supports the need for a redistribution of caring responsibilities between women and men, referring to the need for 'greater solidarity between men and women [being] needed if men are to take on greater responsibility for the caring role in our societies' (European Commission, 1994).

Within this clear EU policy context, the EC Childcare Network undertook a programme of work between 1991 and 1996 on the theme of 'men as carers'. This programme covered a European seminar held in Ravenna in 1993, and the publication of several reports, including *Men as Workers in Childcare Services*, written by Jytte Jensen (1995), the Danish member of the Network. In most of these reports, the theme of men as carers covered both fathers *and* men working in services for young children.

The Thomas Coram Research Unit Project

In London in 1996, the Thomas Coram Research Unit (TCRU) began a project concerned with the workforce in English day care services in general, and the issue of men working in these services in particular ('day care services' means those services within the split system of early childhood services in the UK which fall within the welfare system, such as day nurseries, childminders and playgroups; the term 'early childhood services' includes both day care services and services for children under five which fall within the education system, such as nursery classes, nursery schools and reception classes). The Council Recommendation on Childcare provided part of the background to the project, but other more specifically UK considerations were equally important.

In recent years, there has been a rapid increase in the UK both in the number of day care services and in the number of workers employed in these services, in particular in private day nurseries and as childminders; for example, in England the number of places in private day nurseries increased more than fivefold between 1986 and 1996 and the number of places at childminders increased nearly threefold (Department of Health, 1997a: Table 1). In terms of setting the UK in context, it should be emphasized that day care policy in the UK, unlike for example the Nordic countries, is that services should usually be provided privately and paid for by parents; only a small proportion of children are entitled to day care services at public expense and less than 5 per cent of services are either publicly provided or publicly funded.

Despite the recent rapid expansion of private market services and previous research pointing to a strong relationship between staffing and the quality of services, there has been little research undertaken in this country on the workforce in day care or other early childhood services. This is even more true of the gender dimension within the workforce, despite the fact that work in day care services remains one of the most female dominated of all occupations. (For a review of the literature on the workforce in day care services in Britain and five other countries, see Cameron, 1997; for a review of the literature on gender in childcare work, see Cameron, submitted.)

The TCRU project on the workforce in day care services involves the following pieces of work.

- A secondary analysis of the Labour Force Survey (LFS), a large government survey conducted every quarter, which has helped to build up a picture of the overall workforce in UK early childhood services, including the proportion of men, and to make comparisons with some other occupations involving children or caring work. A summary of some of the main results from this secondary analysis can be found in the Appendix to this chapter, showing for example the very high level of gender segregation among staff working in day care services (96 per cent or more are women), which is equalled or surpassed by the other occupations only by midwives. Although these results refer to the UK, in principle it should be possible to undertake similar analyses in other countries, as the LFS is conducted in all other European countries.
- A survey of the 350 further education colleges in England training nursery workers explored gender issues in training.
- A survey of all English local authorities asked about their policies concerning men working in day care services.
- A study was made of ten centres which employ at least one male worker, involving in-depth interviews with a male and female worker in each centre in order to explore and contrast their experience and attitudes, and shorter interviews with a selection of parents in order to explore their views about male workers. It is instructive that in the course of this study and all the other work undertaken over the last two years, the research team has only found one centre in the whole of England – the Sheffield Children's Centre (see the Chapters 15 and 20) – which can be said to have a mixed gender workforce, with roughly equal numbers of men and women workers. Otherwise, where men are employed, they come in ones or, exceptionally, twos.

One purpose on organizing the seminar was to take forward the work being undertaken at the TCRU. Another purpose was to contribute to cross-national working, by providing a forum in which to share and exchange experience, knowledge and perspectives between participants from six countries. In this way, it is hoped that the seminar takes forward the work of the EC Childcare Network, and more generally the 'European' discussion about more equal sharing of care between men and women and the role of men as carers for children.

The different discourses

The title of the seminar – 'Men as Workers in Services for Young Children: Issues of a Mixed-gender Workforce' – reflected a growing awareness that the issue of men in services for young children cannot be studied in isolation. The question of why so few men work in these services can only be answered by asking other questions, in particular 'Why are there so many women working in this field?' and 'Why does caring, in its broadest sense, remain such gendered work?'. These questions lead to even more fundamental questions about the purpose of services for young children, the nature of the work in these services and the knowledge and qualities needed to undertake the work. One reading of the heavily gendered nature of work in day care services is that these services are widely understood as substitute homes and the work as substitute mothering, drawing on what some would view as women's innate child-rearing instincts.

Furthermore, any increase in the number of male workers in early childhood services has implications for women workers and for mothers, as well as, of course, for fathers and children. No-one, as far as we know, advocates moving from the extreme of a very high proportion of women workers in this occupation to the opposite extreme of a very high proportion of men workers; instead what is envisaged is a more evenly balanced workforce. The issue, therefore, is not just about the conse-quences of more male workers but also the consequences of moving from a gendered occupation to a mixed gender occupation.

There is also increasing awareness that the issue under study can be, and is, discussed within the context of a number of different discourses. The European Union (EU) mainly locates its interest within a *gender equality discourse*. More equal sharing of childcare between women and men, with men necessarily assuming greater responsibility, is seen by the EU as one of a number of necessary conditions for achieving one of its major stated policy objectives, namely equal treatment for women in the labour market. Although the EU does not specifically apply this discourse to men working in services with children, some would see this as part of a wider approach to promoting equal opportunities by offering boys and girls examples of men adopting caring roles and responsibilities, rather than reinforcing more traditional gender roles and responsibilities.

> To bring children up with a sense of equality demands that pedagogues respect and value all children and their individual needs. They must also create stimulating environments inside as well as outside for these different needs. At the same time, the pedagogues must be aware of the gender of the children in their choice of activities. Probably these policies and recommendations can more easily be fulfilled by a mixed-gender work group that will contain a greater diversity of masculine and feminine traits than a single-gender group. A single-gender group has greater difficulty in treating children equally and 'educating' them in equality – because children do not do what we say they should do, but they do what they see we do. (Jensen, 1995: 21)

From this perspective, nurseries and other early childhood services are understood to be community institutions and public spaces which undertake projects of social and cultural significance, including the co-construction, by children and workers, of gender identity; and, as such, the gender mix of the staff is significant for this process of co-construction. More generally, it might be argued that the absence or presence of men in early childhood services contributes to or challenges dominant ideologies about gender roles and relationships in the wider community. A centre with a mixed-gender workforce, for example, is part of a gender equality discourse, including equal sharing of childcare between women and men, just as a centre with only women workers is part of a very different discourse which identifies women as particularly suited to caring for children.

A second discourse concerns the labour market and its structuring. In this *labour market discourse*, the workforce in early childhood services is just one example of the operation of occupational segregation in the labour market, which is seen as a rigidity in the operation of the market which hampers its efficient functioning. Issues here include the causes of occupational segregation, the consequences, what conditions may promote desegregation and the consequences of men entering female-dominated occupations and *vice versa*.

The third discourse may broadly be labelled the *children's needs discourse* – or 'for the sake of the children'. It addresses the benefits to children of having a mixed-gender workforce. One strand of this discourse concerns the idea that male workers in early childhood services provide 'role models' to children in a world in which men, and especially fathers, are often and increasingly absent or marginal in the children's lives. This is because increasing numbers of children live in families affected by the highest level of lone parenthood in the EU and the longest working hours for employed fathers.

The other strand concerns 'gender difference', the view that there are gendered differences between boys and girls, and that if boys and girls are to have their needs fully met, then they require early childhood workers who can recognize, reflect and respond to these gender differences. The 'gender difference' view has been influential in Denmark, as described by Jytte Jensen in her report for the EC Childcare Network:

> The fact that boys and girls are different in some ways and choose different games and activities gives different challenges to those employed – both female and male – in childcare centres. The daily pedagogic work must take these differences into account if the needs of both boys and girls are to be covered. In Denmark today, some childcare services work consciously with gender pedagogy in which it is emphasized that specific gender behaviour must be reflected in pedagogic work ... irrespective of the gender of the staff. (Jensen, 1995: 20)

The fourth discourse might be called the *risk and child protection discourse*. It draws on the idea that children can be at risk of abuse or exploitation from adults, especially men, both in the home and in services. This opens up a discussion of how best to protect children against this risk, ranging from introducing special practices to prohibiting the employment of male workers.

Of course, there is some overlap between these discourses. For example, occupational segregation is an issue in the labour market discourse because it leads to inefficient use of human resources, but it also has specific gender equality dimensions concerning exclusion from employment opportunities (although, with respect to the subject of this book, the interest in occupational segregation as a gender issue has been more focused on women entering male-dominated occupations than men entering female-dominated occupations). Acceptance of 'gender difference' leads to the view that children *need* a mixed gender workforce and that genuine gender *equality* requires recognition of difference rather than sameness; genuine gender equality, just like genuine ethnic equality, will come through treating children and adults as equal but different rather than treating people as if they were all essentially the same.

As well as overlaps, there are also tensions between some of these discourses. Employing more male workers to meet the needs of children may give rise to concerns that it might undermine the employment position of women in early childhood services. Ambivalence about the employment of more men also has a role to play within the risk and child protection discourse.

The organizers of the seminar tried to recognize all of these discourses in the seminar programme, and this is reflected in this book and in the range of the participants invited. However, it is also necessary to recognize that different discourses are prioritized in different countries. The seminar and this book provide an opportunity to explore these differences, and the reasons for them. Indeed one reason why cross-national work is so important is that it enables us to understand better and to question more deeply the situation and the discourses in our own countries, which we often take for granted. Similarly, introducing gender into early childhood services allows problematization and deconstruction of many of the assumptions and practices of these services and of work with young children, rendering the invisible visible and the unquestioned questionable.

The issues from a British perspective

As just noted, different discourses dominate in different countries. For example, from various sources (including the discussions at the seminar), it seems that whereas the 'children's needs' discourse is quite prominent in the Nordic countries, it figures little in Britain, where the issue of gender receives far less attention in early childhood policy and practice than, for example, ethnicity (as can be seen in the relative attention paid to gender and ethnicity in the Children Act 1989 and the accompanying volumes of guidance and regulations). Instead, two discourses predominate in Britain: 'risk and child protection' (also very prominent in the United States, but much less so in the Nordic countries) and 'gender equality'.

This chapter concludes with an examination of these two discourses in more detail, drawing on the findings from the survey of further education colleges in England training nursery workers. The survey was addressed to staff in colleges offering the CACHE Diploma in Nursery Nursing and the BTEC Diploma in Early Childhood Studies, and asked a series of questions on issues of gender on childcare courses. We received 269 completed questionnaires, a response rate of 54 per cent. Only 3 per cent of respondents were men and only 1.2 per cent of students enrolled on full-time courses were men.

The gender equality discourse

The legislative basis for a concern with equality between the sexes in Britain is the Sex Discrimination Act 1975 and the Equal Pay Act 1970. the task of implementing these measures was given to Equal Opportunities Commission, set up in December 1975. Parliament gave the Commission a duty to promote, monitor and enforce the sex equality laws with the aim of addressing the evident inequalities between men and women in pay and opportunities in education and employment, and beyond that in all spheres of life. However, this goal has not yet been achieved. Twenty years after the legislation, for example, inequalities exist in the average income of men and women, and the labour market is still strongly segregated (see Table 2.1). At the extremes, childcare, consists of 98 per cent women workers, while building workers are 99 per cent men.

Table 2.1 Gender differences in income and occupation	
Gross weekly earnings for men aged 30–49:	£735
Gross weekly earnings for women aged 30–49:	£455
Source: EOC, 1995	
Proportion of LFS occupations with between 40 and 60 percent male and female:	12%
Source: Labour Force Survey, 1991–1995	

Equality between men and women within households has also been a subject of concern. For example, men's participation in the traditionally female world of the domestic and childcare workload of running family life is seen to be undergoing change and is subject to scrutiny. Studies indicate that while women remain very much the main carers for children, whether or not they are employed outside the home, men are contributing more to both housework and childcare. Some previously 'women only' domains, such as childbirth, are now regularly, normatively, witnessed by fathers.

As a result of growing moves towards equality of opportunity at work, in training and within households, the concept of promoting equality of opportunity is now firmly embedded within many work and training environments, such as the curriculum of childcare courses and the selection procedure in training colleges. A survey of college lecturers frequently referred to the curriculum guidelines given by the leading awarding body, CACHE (Council for Awards in Children's Care and Education). These state that:

> The Board desires to promote equality of opportunity and anti-discriminatory practices and so help to eradicate negative stereotyping attitudes and practices in relation to age, being a gay man or lesbian woman, class, disability, employment status, gender, health, marital status, race and religion.

Also in the realm of services for young children, the volume of guidance and regulations accompanying the Children Act 1989 relevant to day care services referred to the principle of *diversity* in children and the need to *value individuals* and their backgrounds. This principle was more highly developed in relation to race and ethnicity than to gender. It stated that:

> People working with young children should value and respect the different racial origins, religions, cultures and languages in a multi-racial society so that each child is valued as an individual without racial or gender stereotyping. (Department of Health, 1991: para. 6.10)

Responses in the survey of college tutors overwhelmingly supported the idea of men working alongside women in childcare establishments (see Table 2.2). They saw the involvement of men as workers in terms of reflecting society and reflecting (idealized) family life, where men and women both figure and take responsibility for children. They saw it in terms of challenging gender stereotypes in the work environment, so that childcare did not continue to be seen as 'women's work' and, thus, would benefit the profession (no longer so devalued). They also saw the employment of male childcare workers as important for supplying positive male role models to children. Sometimes this was seen in terms of

Table 2.2 Percentages in favour of each gender mix and the reasons given
Questions: Would you prefer nursery nursing to have a mixed-gender workforce of to continue as a predominantly female professions?

Mixed gender	86%
Predominantly female profession	6%
Reason for preferring a mixed gender workforce	
Provide positive role models for children	18%
Provide compensatory role models	8%
Benefit the profession	7%
Reflect changing society	2%
Reduce stereotyping and prejudice	2%

Source: Survey of childcare lecturers, Thomas Coram Research Unit, 1996

children from single parent families, where it was assumed that children do not often see men, and sometimes in terms of role models for boys, who were thought to benefit from an additional gender dimension in staffing childcare services.

Although the equality discourse appeared to predominate in the responses of college lecturers, there was little indication that they had been, or were being successful in measures to address recruitment. Few respondents said their colleges specifically aimed recruitment at male students. Less than 2 per cent of students in the responding colleges were male. Furthermore, no consensus emerged on the means of recruiting more male students to childcare courses. Many respondents did not know or were looking for suggestions themselves as to how to recruit more men. It would appear that while the principle of equality between the sexes in childcare work is firmly in place, the means of achieving a mixed-gender workforce through recruitment to training colleges needs urgent attention.

In summary, there is a discourse of gender equality in Britain. It has been interpreted as equality of opportunity for all. Within childcare colleges, the principle is interpreted as non-discrimination rather than the more active concern of establishing equality between the sexes in the workforce. At a national level, government and public bodies such as the Equal Opportunities Commission have adopted a cautious approach to the issue. Consequently, the gender equality discourse has led to neither a strong commitment to a more gender-mixed childcare workforce, nor to any positive measures to promote this objective.

The risk and child protection discourse

The equality discourse represents the penetration of the childcare world with wider concerns about gender equality. The risk discourse, however, can be seen as a central policy concern within children's services influencing the wider world. The concept of 'risk', in other words, was initially the way welfare services perceived their role with children, but has grown to become an issue within services, within families and on the streets of Britain. How has this evolved alongside the equality discourse?

The management of risk has been the central preoccupation of social welfare services for children in Britain. In the post-war era this has become more confidently articulated to mean the 'risk' of a child being abused, and the necessary measures to 'protect' children from abuse. Various examples can be given of the way the idea of 'risk' has come to dominate the child welfare discourse. The origin of the risk discourse can be seen in English law and in policies developed by welfare agencies in order to protect children. For example, a register of children 'at risk' is a central means for welfare agencies to identify particular children. This focus on individual children was highlighted during the 1980s, when there were a number of high-profile enquiries into the circumstances of deaths of children who were under the supervision of welfare agencies (e.g. Beckford, 1985; Henry, 1987; and Carlisle, 1987).

This concern with identification of risk has grown beyond risk in domestic situations to risk in other spheres. During the 1990s, children were seen to be at risk within the services they attended for their welfare and safety. Several notorious cases highlighted this risk. For example, Frank Beck was imprisoned in 1992 for a long history of offences against children committed while employed by local authorities to work in children's homes. In early 1997 Keith Laverack was similarly found guilty of offences against children, this time as part of a large paedophile ring. In early childhood services, in 1994 Jason Dabbs, a nursery nurse student, pleaded guilty to charges of sexual abuse against more than 60 children attending nursery education classes. In 1996, 16 children and their teacher were murdered while inside their primary school by a man, Thomas Hamilton, who had been known to police for suspected paedophile activities. Also in 1996, a man ran amok in a nursery class playground with a machete, injuring several children and their nursery nurse.

Widespread publicity has also been given to violent crimes against children committed in public. For example, in 1993, Jamie Bulger, a two-year-old, was abducted while shopping with his parents by a pair of ten year old boys and murdered by them. In 1995, a long history of adult abduction, torture and murder by one married couple, Fred and Rosemary West, was uncovered. Over a 20-year period they had enticed young women into their home, killed them and buried them under the floorboards. In 1996, news of a Belgian paedophile ring involving the abduction and murder of young girls was given wide publicity in Britain. In August of that year, the *Observer* newspaper ran the headline 'Are our children safe on the streets?'.

An analysis of stories in the home news sections of two national newspapers, the *Guardian* and the *Observer*, including the words 'men' and 'children' in the same paragraph, in 1996, revealed 78 stories, 39 of which involved men taking responsibility for children. Of these, 26 were concerned with violent behaviour towards children (see Table 2.3).

What does this risk discourse mean for men working with young children?

• The central preoccupation with the protection of children has extended beyond protecting children from risk in their own homes and from strangers on the streets, to workers employed within services.

Table 2.3 Newspaper stories including 'men' and 'children' in the same paragraph, 1996 (*The Guardian* and T*he Observer*) (excluding those in which men's behaviour or roles were not seen as responsible for the story)

Men's roles with and attitudes towards children	
Changing roles in society (e.g. new man)	5
Changing roles at work (e.g. male teachers in decline)	1
Fatherhood	3
Total	9
Health and social issues	
Malnutrition	1
Child circumcision	1
The father's role in health matters	2
Total	4
Men's violent behaviour towards children	
Rape and sex offenders	2
Residential care and sexual abuse	5
Child murder/massacre	3
Child contact/domestic violence	3
Pornography/prostitution/paedophilia	13
Total	26

- Men are identified as a greater risk to children than women (Finklehor, Williams and Burns, 1988).
- Young children are thought to be more vulnerable than old children. Children under the age of five are more frequently subject to registration on the child protection register than older age groups (Department of Health, 1997a) and are more likely to be the subject of care applications by local authorities (Brophy, Wale and Bates, 1997).

In sum, the risk discourse creates a fearful environment for working with children, particularly with young children, and particularly for men. Some institutions have responded to the fearfulness by formalising procedures, or by developing specific protective practices, such as witnessing policies, where two people will always change a child's nappy. Others have pointed out how risky this is for the remaining group of children, who may be left relatively unsupervised while two members of staff are out of the room.

The risk discourse is one outcome of a construction of the welfare services around individual rather than universal entitlement to services, but it is not only this. Several other factors might be considered. For example, it may be that the way gender roles have been constructed in relation to children over time and in the contemporary period – so that men have traditionally been peripheral carers of children, but central material providers – has contributed to the idea that children can be 'legitimate' subjects for men's violence. Or it may be that the currently precarious social cohesion of society provides the opportunities for disaffected, devalued people with violent tendencies to find children easy prey both within and outside their homes.

Alternatively, the risk discourse could be seen as part of a generative news agenda. Burgess (1997) points out that newspaper stories about male violence towards children make the news precisely because the events are rare, rather than because they are ordinary. However, the fact of their newsworthiness contributes not to eliminating the risk discourse, but to policy initiatives, commentary, practices and research that investigate and seek to manage perceptions of risk to children.

Table 2.4 Percentages of respondents who identified these advantages of a mixed-gender workforce

	%
Offers positive role model to children	98
Offers children the opportunity to see men and women working together	95
Challenges gender stereotypes	85
Better able to respond to gender diversity among children	73

Source: Survey of childcare lecturers, Thomas Coram Research Unit, 1996

Conclusions

The survey of lecturers in colleges showed that nearly all respondents wanted childcare to become a more mixed-gender profession (see Table 2.4). Against this firm commitment to the idea of equality between the sexes in the staffing of childcare services, several factors emerged which served to complicate such an idea becoming a reality. First, over half thought that women's careers would suffer as a consequence of employing men as men would be more likely to take the senior positions. Second, as already reported above, many respondents saw the important issue of recruitment as outside their control, or were bereft of ideas as to how to affect change in their recruitment patterns. Third, the issue of risk to children through male employment in childcare services was significant. About one-third of respondents saw no connection between increasing numbers of male workers and increasing reports of child abuse. Over half, on the other hand, thought either that measures such as screening recruits and policies to safeguard children would be necessary, or that they were unsure, or that there was a definite relationship between male workers and cases of abuse. Some respondents said that as women abuse too, introducing more men would not make any difference. Taken together, these responses indicate a climate, among childcare lecturers, of *fear* of risk of abuse in childcare settings, and some association of risk with male workers.

Childcare lecturers could be seen as an exemplar for wider society and for the equality discourse. There is, we believe, wide support for the idea of men as workers in childcare services. However, within the gender equality discourse there is a piece missing – and that piece is the issue of gender as relevant to young children's services in the public mind. There is, however, a powerful counterforce in existence, represented by the risk discourse. The pervasiveness of perceptions of risk acts as a barrier to the fulfilment of childcare lecturers' ambitions.

One of the challenges in Britain today is to explore how these competing discourses can be both respected and challenged, so as to achieve, eventually, a more 'gender aware' childcare profession, in which the needs of, and differences between, children, workers and parents are valued and the service as a whole is confident of its project.

References

Brophy, J., Wale, C. and Bates, P. (1997), *Training and Support in the Guardian ad Litem and Reporting Officer Service*. London: Department of Health.

Burgess, A. (1997), *Fatherhood Reclaimed*. London: Vermilion.

Cameron, C. (1997), 'Review of staffing in childcare centres in six countries', *Early Childhood Care and Development*, 137, 47–67.

— (submitted for publication), 'Promise or problem? A review of the literature of men working in childcare services'.

Department of Health (1991), *The Children Act 1989 Guidance and Regulations: Volume 2, Family Support, Day Care and Educational Provision for Young Children*. London: HMSO.

— (1997a), *Children's Day Care Facilities at 31 March 1996, England*. London: Department of Health.

— (1997b), *Children Looked After By Local Authorities*. London: Department of Health.

European Commission (EC), Childcare Network (European Commission Network on Childcare and other Measures to Reconcile Employment and Family Responsibilities) (1996), *A Decade of Achievement*. Brussels: European Commission Equal Opportunities Unit.

— (Directorate-General for Employment, Industrial Relations and Social Affairs) (1993), *European Social Policy: Options for the Union (Green Paper)*. Luxembourg: Office for Official Publications of the European Communities.

— (Directorate-General for Employment, Industrial Relations and Social Affairs) (1994), *European Social Policy: A Way Forward for the Union (White Paper)*. Luxembourg: Office for Official Publications of the European Communities.

Finkelhor, D., Williams, L.M. and Burns, N. (1988), *Nursery Crimes: Sexual Abuse in Day care*. Newbury Park, CA: Sage.

Jensen, J. (1995), *Men as Workers for Children: A Discussion Paper for the EC Childcare Network*. Brussels: European Commission Equal Opportunities Unit.

Appendix
The Childcare Workforce in Britain:
Data from the Labour Force Survey

The Labour Force Survey

The Labour Force Survey (LFS) is a national survey of private households throughout Great Britain. It collects data from approximately 60,000 households per quarter. The survey is conducted by the Office for National Statistics. Data are collected on a wide range of subjects, including occupation, training, marital status and household composition. For the 1991 Census a new occupational classification was introduced and this is also used by the LFS.

Standard Occupational Classification

The Standard Occupational Classification is a detailed classification of occupations. It is an hierarchical classification with nine major groups, 87 minor groups and hundreds of unit groups. Unit groups are sets of specific occupations, grouped together on the basis of the tasks performed and on similarities of qualifications, training, skills and experience commonly associated with those tasks. One minor group is called Childcare and Related Occupations.

Childcare and Related Occupations
Childcare and related workers supervise play and other activities for pre-school age children, assist teachers with their non-teaching duties and care for children in day or residential nurseries, children's homes and private households. (Office of Population Censuses and Surveys, 1990, *Standard Occupational Classification, Vol. 1*: 204)

Table A The childcare workforce in Britain: data from the Labour Force Survey

	Female %	Under 26 %	White %	Single %	Mean hours	Temporary %	Shifts %	Qualifications %		
								Degree	Prof/Voc	None
Nursery nurses	99.2	32.8	95.5	32.3	33.4	10.8	16.3	1.0	74.9	5.2
Playgroup leaders	97.1	4.5	97.4	6.8	17.5	5.9	3.9	3.6	62.5	9.4
Educational assistants	96.4	8.4	97.5	9.1	23.7	28.6	1.0	4.6	41.0	23.4
Other childcare	98.0	17.7	97.6	16.8	30.4	14.5	3.8	1.7	33.2	33.4
Primary teachers	85.7	5.4	98.2	13.2	42.1	16.1	0.3	45.6	52.8	0.4
Secondary teachers	53.9	3.9	97.5	13.9	43.6	11.1	0.3	76.2	23.1	0.2
Social workers	75.6	5.2	93.1	15.4	41.2	4.8	26.6	28.2	42.4	13.5
Nurses	90.6	10.6	92.8	16.6	37.0	6.8	66.5	4.8	89.3	1.5
Midwives	98.4	7.1	89.3	19.8	36.9	4.9	75.3	4.7	91.9	0.2

Source: Labour Force Survey, 1991–1995 (spring quarter)
©*Data are Crown Copyright and are used with permission*

It is not clear from this definition, but it would seem that care is not confined to preschool-age children. The group includes four unit groups: Nursery Nurses, Playgroup Leaders, Educational Assistants, and Other Childcare and Related Occupations. This last group includes such jobs as *au pairs*, child minders and nannies. This minor group does not include nursery teachers: these are classified with other teachers, and appear in the same unit group as primary school teachers, for children aged 5–11.

Childcare workforce

The Table below shows a number of characteristics of the childcare workforce in Britain, along with the same data for a number of other occupations also concerned with the care of children: primary and nursery teachers, secondary teachers, social workers, nurses and midwives. It can be seen that the childcare workforce is predominantly female, well over 97 per cent – about the same as midwives. There are fewer female nursery and primary teachers and even fewer female social workers, but not all social workers have contact with children, and it may be that those who do are more likely to be female. Childcare workers are young, especially nursery nurses (32.8 per cent are aged under 26), much younger than the other groups. The proportion who are white is much the same as for the population as a whole (95 per cent): only midwives have a noticeably lower percentage. Almost one-third of nursery nurses are single – twice the percentage for nurses – but very few playgroup leaders are (6.8 per cent).

Nursery nurses work on average 33.4 hours per week; as some are working part time, others must be working longer hours. There is a similar percentage of childcare workers whose jobs are temporary as there are teachers, but more than for social workers, nurses or midwives. Many nursery nurses work shifts (16.3 per cent), but few other childcare workers do so. Few nursery nurses or playgroup leaders have no qualifications, most having a professional or vocational qualification of some kind. Few have degrees. Educational assistants and other childcare workers are more likely to have no formal qualifications.

PART 2

Non-traditional Working:
What happens when men move into
female-dominated occupations?

3 What happens when men move into female-dominated occupations?

Erna Sundqvist
Gothenburg, Sweden

Introduction

When I began to look at men moving into female-dominated occupations, I had several projects behind me, mostly in the field of industrial organization, but all involving the division of labour and the effects of gender on job seniority. As a sociologist, my research has been about communication, structure and power.

The project discussed below was initiated by the Equal Rights Board in Gothenburg, Sweden, in 1988, and it was to set up the Equal Rights Childcare Centre. The Centre was to have as many men as women employees and the goal was to create a workplace that could be considered 'equal' by the workers, children and parents. The issue of equal rights was to be clearly stated. There were two groups of children at the centre and they had four or five staff members in each group. I interviewed some of the teachers, both women and men, at the Equal Rights Centre who previously only had experience of working groups dominated by females. Some of the female teachers had never worked with a trained male teacher. In total I interviewed 11 male and 25 female teachers. I worked with the Equal Rights Centre for one year.

The research took work organization as its starting point. I wanted to find out what happens when males enter a female group and especially a group whose task was to do the most female task in society, namely taking care of children. Some of the starting questions were, What kind of men are there at the Centre?'; 'What do they say about themselves and each other?'; and 'What do the women think about the men entering their field of competence?'. I went on to ask, 'What happens in a female organization when a lot of males enter it?'.

Although the children and their parents were not my primary focus, I met many parents and had some very interesting discussions with them concerning their views of this special Centre. For that reason, they were given a special chapter in the report. The children were around us the whole time, and, in one sense, they have the leading role, so it was natural to include them too.

I have three children of my own, all have been at the community child-care centre. They, and I as a parent, have some experience of men as teachers, but none of them have been to a centre like this.

This chapter focuses on:

- the work organization and the relations between the staff members;
- the kind of men I met;
- the relations with the children and their parents.

How is the work organized?

First I want to point out the small scale of this project. It is only one centre, and a centre which received a lot of positive support just because it focused on the issue of being an equal rights centre. However, I did follow the Centre for a whole year and compared it to some other centres.

The Centre had very few conflicts, and those that did occur were resolved more quickly than they would have been at other centres where the employees had worked before. This was the opinion of both the women and men who worked there.

The women adopted more or less the men's way of speaking to each other, which was described by the women as a more direct way. You might think that they subordinated themselves, but the women never considered it that way. They had thought it over, they had many years of experience of talking their own way which they said was to go 'round and round', and they found that the way the men talked was better and decided to change. One of the women who changed said, 'Speaking like this to each other, is more like the way I talk to my husband and children at home.' For me, as an equal rights supporter, this sounds great and I really wish changes like this could happen once in a male-dominated group!

The employees said that conversation between the staff members was different compared to the centres they had worked in before. Both the women and the men in this group said it was fun and easy to talk to each other. The group in the Equal Rights Centre, compared to the other groups, broadened the topics of conversation with new subjects such as politics and sports. All these subjects were introduced by the men and we can call them the 'men's subjects', but it is important to see that this is the first time that they had been able to talk about such subjects in their own working team. All the men and most of the women enjoyed these new subjects. Very quickly, the women entered into a discussion of the new subjects. However, I did not find the men doing the same when the women were talking about curtains for the Centre or what they would buy for dinner. That kind of matter the men still called 'women's talk' and they kept quiet.

During the time I was at the Centre, conducting interviews and observing the work, I also had other kinds of meetings with the group. Some were on my own and some were with a male consultant. The aim of these meetings was to train the staff to observe gender roles. This was not without complications. Both the men and the women were very protective of the group: they were reluctant to see the differences among themselves. The men especially had a hard time admitting that they were different: they said that through their education they were exactly the same as the women. I tried to make them recognize the gender roles that they themselves were part of. My ambition was that they should recognize bad gender patterns in themselves both in the working group and when acting together with the children.

At the end of the year, the group was more conscious of the differences and of the negative patterns, and they were much more aware of the differences in the way they wanted to tackle them. The women decided, for example, not to stop talking 'women's talk', as they preferred to do when they were by themselves. When they were together in the mixed group, they talked what they called 'general subjects'. The men did not change. Nevertheless, after one year, everyone at the Centre said that they had fun coffee breaks and they liked talking to each other.

As stated above, in the beginning the men did not want to see any differences at all but, after discussions about what the group could gain from the differences, the following topics came up:

• most men have something special that they are good at, whereas women are more general;
• women are better at clearing things up;
• women can do more things at the same time without becoming stressed;
• men do not 'nag' so much; they just do it.

These were the men's ideas of the differences. None of the men mentioned that women were better at changing the way they interact, though some of them had mentioned it to me earlier in the discussions.

The women could very quickly, after this year, and without hesitation, bring out the differences between male and female workers. They brought out many positive things about employing men, for example staff co-operation. However, some negative things came up as well:

• men don't see or don't want to see what needs to be done when it comes to cleaning, whether it is the floor or the children's hands;
• men don't want to do the planning.

None of the women mentioned anything they felt that they did better than the men.

All of the staff members liked working together. They described the work situation as something very positive. The women said that this was the first time in their working lives that they had had this feeling of a natural working group. They liked discussing subjects with the men and they shared a lot of jokes. Neither the men nor the women wanted to go back to a female-dominated workplace. When we were talking about the climate in the group, everyone in the staff said that the female leader of the group – Monica Everts – was the best leader they had ever had. Monica Everts is still the leader of the group and in an interview I conducted with her recently – now eight years since the Centre was set up – she stated that the situation there was still as good. There were still as many men as women at the centre. All had children of their own and three of the men had been there for a long time, two nearly from the beginning. The parents were very satisfied with the whole Centre and there was a waiting list for children to enter.

The structure of the organization from the beginning was very open, everybody helped each other. Every staff member had responsibility for at least one thing. I found the group very free from boring routines and less bureaucratic than the others I have met. It was possible to do most things without any problems.

What kind of men were there at the Centre, and what kind of men choose to work with young children?

The answer is: no special kind, they were all different. They had varied attitudes to the children, to other men, to the conditions of working life and so on. I want to emphasize this so it does not give the impression that all men are like this or like that. This is important to me, because many of the women who had not worked with, or who had had very little contact with, male teachers had a very stereotypical image of who these men were. The most common opinion was that they were gay, that they were not real men, not strong and practical and that they did not understand children as well as the women did. However, they acknowledged that the men were good for the boys.

Of course the men were similar to them in some ways. For example they had all worked with children before they were trained as teachers; they all liked the work and thought that work with children was an important task; and they liked the freedom of the job and none of them felt less masculine because of their job. All the employees, both men and women said that the wages were far too low and the men mentioned their social status quite often. Many of them expressed that a desire to develop their jobs and, for example, to work with music, woodwork and special nature projects. The female teachers also wanted to work with special projects, but they did not express it in the same way as the men.

None of the men had experienced resistance from their spouses, but some had received negative comments from their own parents such as, 'I always tried to make you a proper man.'

When the group moved into the Centre, the building was not yet finished and there were still many workers in the building. One day, one of the carpenters asked a male teacher, 'What do you really do in there all day? Do you have to change their nappies?' The man answered, 'Yes, indeed.' The carpenter looked back and said, 'It's a hell of an important job you're doing. I wish my children could have both men and women around them.'

Relations with parents

I think that the greatest difference in attitude from the parents when comparing this centre to others, are the fathers. It was amazing to see how many of the fathers came to the Centre with a very relaxed attitude. They talked about boots that were too small, the colds and boys fighting, in the same way as the mothers did. The fathers liked to meet the men and sometimes they found themselves involved in a soccer discussion, but they also talked about the children's playground or if their baby had had a good day.

Two of the parents were negative in the beginning, they were both single mothers with young daughters. Their worries disappeared after a short time.

It is illuminating here to recount a story that some of the female teachers told me when they explained the differences in attitudes towards the parents. One of the fathers was what we might call a mild alcoholic. The staff discussed the situation, and no-one wanted to talk to the father. One afternoon when the father came in and was drunk, one of the male teachers became so upset and angry that he went directly to the father and said to him, 'How dare you come here drunk. Damn you, if you come in here one more time and smell of alcohol... .' He put the father in front of him and opened the door. After that he dressed the child and gave him to the father who was waiting outside. It took three weeks before the father returned and after this incident he never came to the Centre drunk. Everyone at the Centre, both the staff and the parents, thought that everybody gained from this solution and especially the child.

The men with the children

I found the men's comments about the children thought-provoking, touching and, now and then, a bit frightening. Some of the men felt that the children were 'thirsting' after them, explaining this reaction as that 'the children have no close contact with other men'. Some children felt uncertain and did not know how to act with men around. The men stated:

At one place where I worked, there were many single mothers. One of the girls asked me if she could call me Daddy. But I felt this was wrong. Later I heard her tell children outside the Centre that her father worked at the Centre.

When I was wrestling with some of the children, I felt strongly that what they really wanted was to hug and to be close, but they didn't dare to seek that kind of contact.

The team spent many hours discussing how to support the children in the right way; how to take advantage of the privileged situation of having both men and women with the children all day long. The female teachers supported the men and mentioned many positive effects that the men had in relation to the children:

- they are positive male role models;
- it is good for all the children who do not have present fathers to meet caring men;
- men play tougher games, such as wrestling and ball games;
- men are seen to be harder than women, tease more and try to toughen the children up;
- men show the children another way to talk.

Together the male and female teachers demonstrated to the children how adults show each other respect, how they work together and can have a lot of fun. They showed the children how to make contact and how to give love, sometimes in different ways.

To conclude, from the beginning this childcare centre was a very good working environment. I believe the most important reasons were that the staff had a very good leader and that they all had something in common. They focused on something they all felt was important, namely women and men working together with young children.

Another important thing was that the women were strong and had a powerful identity at work: they never felt subordinated and they never let the men change something they did not feel was right. They were, or became, more conscious of the gender roles and the women said the men would not gain anything if they lost this equal way of working.

I would argue that it is not enough to have some men in the group, you also have to develop the organization and all the members in a conscious way. You do not get good results only by putting some men into the group. To change old male and female role patterns, we must support both men and women. If we want to see young men able to show the world caring skills, and young girls allowed to develop their self-identity, we have a long way to go. However, we can begin this journey with mixed, conscious working groups for young children.

4 Men in female-dominated occupations in Finland

Johanna Lammi-Taskula
Stakes (National Research and Development Centre for Welfare and Health),
Helsinki, Finland

This chapter looks at the question of what happens when men move into female-dominated occupations from the Nordic, especially Finnish, perspective. The focus is mainly on the social relations and dynamics between male and female colleagues in female-dominated workplaces. It uses empirical data (surveys and interviews) on male kindergarten teachers collected by myself in Finland in 1991 and refers to other research completed in Finland, Sweden and Norway on male nurses and kindergarten teachers. The studies from Sweden and Norway are mainly undergraduate dissertations by students in nursing and pedagogical education, written in native languages.

According to Yvonne Hirdman, when men enter female areas, they quickly rise to the top positions 'like cream' (1990, ref. in Rantalaiho and Heiskanen, 1997). Compared to their female colleagues, men in female-dominated occupations more frequently hold supervisory and administrative positions and, thus, also have higher salaries (Kauppinen-Toropainen and Lammi, 1993). However, if we compare these men to other men in typical male-dominated occupations, we find that the token men in female-dominated occupations earn significantly less (Kauppinen, Haavio-Mannila and Kandolin, 1989). The economic aspect is one of the reasons why men have been less eager than women to cross over gender barriers in working life. However, money does not mean everything. Another important block to men's crossing over is stereotypical masculinity that is vulnerable to stigmatization and prejudices of not being a 'real man' (Williams, 1989; and Bradley, 1993). Where do these prejudices come from? I think they are part of the present male-dominated gender system, where the basic dimensions are difference and hierarchy (Hirdman, 1990, ref. in Rantalaiho and Heiskanen, 1997).

The 'difference' means that men and women should be clearly distinct categories. Maintaining this difference to women is more important to men than *vice versa*, both socially and psychologically. This has to do with the principle of 'hierarchy', which means that everything that is categorized as female or feminine has less cultural prestige than that which is categorized as male or masculine. Men do not choose tradition-ally female occupations because those occupations are not as highly valued in society as traditional male occupations, and because men want to avoid a feminine label that would threaten their masculinity.

Does this mean that we will never see many men in occupations that have for a long time been, and still are, female-dominated? Is there any hope for breaking the gender segregation?

The gender system, with the two dimensions of difference and hierarchy, is not necessarily a universal and everlasting one. Instead, it can be seen as being constantly in the process of reproduction and change. According to Dorothy Smith (1987), social relations are 'always in the making' rather than being fixed. Active subjects shape the structures through practice and action. There are gendering processes going on in working life: the division of labour between men and women is being re-negotiated in everyday life in workplaces. The value given to men's and women's work in society may slowly change as new femininities and masculinities are emerging.

I think it is important to stress that instead of one monolithic mascu-linity there are many different masculinities co-existing. According to Michael S. Kimmel, we live in an era of transition in the definition of masculinity (Kimmel, 1987). Kimmel writes about two parallel tradi-tions, the tension between ambitious breadwinners and compassionate fathers; between Rambo and Phil Donahue. Instead of two masculinities, however, I think we can see an almost endless number of masculinities, produced by combinations of gender, age, race, class, ethnicity, religion, etc., on cultural, historical, interpersonal and psychodynamic levels (Hearn, 1994). This means that in addition to the possible differences between men and women, there are also many differences between men. This should be kept in mind when we discuss gender dynamics in different settings, in this case in workplaces.

In Finland, the proportion of men in female-dominated occupations has been growing since the 1970s, but the change has been very slow (Table 4.1). Men have entered waitering work in restaurants and cafes more than care work in hospitals and kindergartens. Psychiatric nursing is an exception: as in other countries, there is a long tradition in Finland of male nurses working with violent patients that are regarded as too dangerous for women (Williams, 1989; and Sandnes and Tanem, 1991).

When men work in traditionally female occupations, they often do different tasks than their female colleagues. Emphasizing masculinity is a way to create distance from the female colleagues and legitimize working in a female job. In general nursing, men often specialize in 'exciting' areas such as emergency rooms, intensive care and anaesthesia, and they are more interested in technical expertise than in the basic care work (Williams, 1989; and Sandnes and Tanem, 1991). Male nurses are, according to several studies, more interested than women in administrative and managerial work (Soini, 1974; Rosby-Björkquist and Knutsson, 1986; and Carlsson and Bergknut, 1988).

Table 4.1 Percentages of men in female-dominated occupations in Finland, 1970–1993

	1970	1980	1993
Kindergarten teachers	0.2	3.8	4.7
Psychiatric nurses	29.3	31.9	38.5
Registered nurses	0.8	2.2	3.3
Secretaries	4.0	4.8	3.0
Waiters	6.6	12.1	19.1

Source: Statistics Finland, Population Census 1960–1996

The same phenomenon can be seen in the study of male kindergarten teachers in Finland that I conducted in 1991. I collected survey data from 145 respondents and conducted 12 interviews. As the men working in nursery schools face many prejudices questioning their manliness – such as being homosexual, being a 'conchie' (i.e. doing non-military service) or being a lethargic bohemian – they often like to specialize in tasks that can be seen as more masculine. Fewer men work with the very youngest children, they like to arrange sporting and adventurous activities for the older children (Lammi, 1992; Lammi-Taskula, 1993; and Tamminen, 1990).

Many studies have shown that the token in the workplace – the one that is of a different sex to the others – receives a lot of extra attention (Kanter, 1977; Kauppinen-Toropainen, 1987; Tamminen, 1990; and Lammi-Taskula, 1993). Some of the attention is positive and some negative. In kindergartens, men are usually warmly welcomed by women. They are seen as necessary role models for the children, especially for the boys. The male kindergarten teachers are encouraged and supported by the female staff to engage in special, masculine tasks. Thus, both men and women participate in reproducing the gender difference.

If the token man is pushed into a stereotypical masculine role, he can eventually feel frustrated and trapped (Berg, 1980; and Kauppinen-Toropainen, 1987). In the kindergarten, male teachers can, for example, be expected to change light bulbs. Even if certain masculine activities are expected from the men, they should still respect the female working traditions. Thus, some parts of the 'male pedagogy' can cause disagreement. The male kindergarten teachers I studied said they liked to play more rough games with the children: they allowed wrestling, boxing and other physical fighting and let the children take more risks than the women did. This is in conflict with traditional, female pedagogy.

The male kindergarten teachers defined themselves as more relaxed, creative and humorous than the women. They believed they had a normalizing or 'healthy' effect on the social relations of the workplace. As one respondent put it, 'Men bring the principles of fair play with them.' The same notion can be found in other studies of token men in female-dominated workplaces (Carlsson and Bergknut, 1988; and Sandnes and Tanem, 1991). Women are seen by the men as a quarrelling group of hens which need the leadership of a cock.

Token men can be quite lonely in female-dominated workplaces, even if they get along well with their female colleagues. The men feel isolated when the women discuss 'female issues', such as menstruation problems or the prices and quality of stockings. Men think it is easier to communicate with other men, and the token men wish more men were recruited to their workplace. Being the only man in a female-dominated workplace, male hospital nurses seek the company of male doctors (Williams, 1989), and male kindergarten teachers can find a male friend in the caretaker.

Being a token male could be one reason why men in female-dominated occupations are not so eager to stay in the job until retirement (Berg, 1980; Erngren, Birath and Linberg, 1986; Rosby-Björkquist and Knutsson, 1986; Bexell and Söderhamn, 1989; and Sandnes and Tanem, 1991). The men seek career advancement by concentrating on administrative tasks: the basic care work is only a temporary phase for them. Many male kindergarten teachers became kindergarten principals, day care instructors, etc., where the contact with children is not such a central part of the job any more, or they go back to the university to become school teachers.

It can be easy for a young man to play football or wrestle with the children in the kindergarten, but more difficult to imagine doing the same when he is 60 years old. The demarcation of gender difference can be a good coping mechanism for men in female-dominated occupations, but it does not seem to work very well in the long run. A man changes as a person when he moves on in his lifespan. When working in a care profession, interacting daily with other people, and, in the case of kindergarten teachers, interacting with both adults and children, there should be space in the work role to develop together with personal development. A male kindergarten teacher cannot be expected to be the football and wrestling instructor for 40 years.

References

Berg, T.S. (1980), *Mannlige studenter og förskolelärare i studium og yrkesliv*. Bergen Lärerhögskole, förskoleläreravdeling. [*Male students and kindergarten teachers in study and work*. Teachers' College in Bergen. In Norwegian.]

Bradley, H. (1993), 'Across the great divide. The entry of men into "women's jobs"'. In: C.L. Williams (ed.), *Doing 'Women's Work'. Men in Non-traditional Occupations*. Newbury Park: Sage Publications, 10–27.

Carlsson, M. and Bergknut, E. (1988), *Manliga sjuksköterskors syn på sitt yrke*. Vårdhögskolan, Landstinget i Uppsala län. FoU-rapport Nr 2. [*Male nurses' views on their work*. High School of Carework, Uppsala County. In Swedish.]

Erngren, E., Birath, A. and Linberg, L. (1986), *Vart tar de manliga sjukskötarna vägen? En explorativ studie åtta år efter legitimation*. Röda Korsets Sjuksköterskola. [*Where are the male nurses going? A study eight years after graduation*. Red Cross Nursing School. In Swedish.]

Hearn, J. (1994), 'Research in Men and Masculinities: Some Sociological Issues and Possibilities', *Australian and New Zealand Journal of Sociology*, *30*(1).

Kanter, R.M. (1977), *Men and Women of the Corporation*. New York: Basic Books.

Kauppinen, K., Haavio-Mannila, E. and Kandolin, I. (1989), 'Who benefits from working in non-traditional workroles: interaction patterns and quality of worklife', *Acta Sociologica*, *32*(4).

Kauppinen-Toropainen, K. (1987), *Ainokaiset työyhteisössä. Haastattelututkimus työn sukupuolenmukaisen eriytymisen vaikutuksista työtyytyväisyyteen, psyykkiseen uupumukseen ja stressiin*. Työ ja Ihminen, lisänumero 1/87. Helsinki: Työterveyslaitos. [*Tokens in the work community. A survey on the effects of the sex segregation of work on work satisfaction, burnout and stress*. Institute of Occupational Health. In Finnish.]

— and Lammi, J. (1993), 'Men in female-dominated occupations. A cross-cultural comparison'. In: Williams, C.L. (ed.), *Doing 'Women's Work'. Men in Non-traditional Occupations*. Newbury Park: Sage Publications, 91–112.

Kimmel, M.S. (ed.) (1987), *Changing Men. New Directions in Research on Men and Masculinity*. Newbury Park: Sage Publications.

Lammi, J. (1992), *Miehet naisvaltaisissa ammateissa*. Katsaus länsimaisiin julkaisuihin vuosilta 1973–91. Sosiaali- ja terveysministeriö, tasa-arvojulkaisuja. Sarja C: Työraportteja 7/1992. [*Men in female-dominated occupations*. Research review. Ministry of Social Affairs and Health. In Finnish.]

Lammi-Taskula, J. (1993), *Kummajainen vai kunnon mies? Miehet lastentarhanopettajina*. Sosiaali- ja terveysministeriö, tasa-arvojulkaisuja. Sarja C: Työraportteja 7/1993. [*Oddity or a proper man? Men as kindergarten teachers*. Ministry of Social Affairs and Health. In Finnish.]

Rantalaiho, L. and Heiskanen, T. (1997), *Gendered Practices in Working Life*. London: Macmillan Press.

Rosby-Björkquist, E. and Knutsson, G. (1986), *En jämförande studie mellan manliga och kvinnliga sjuksköterskor i vårdarbetet*. Högskolan i Örebro, Institutionen för politik med förvaltning. [*A comparative study of male and female nurses*. High School of Örebro. In Swedish.]

Sandnes, A. and Tanem, T. (1991), 'Frederick Nightingale, I presume?' En undersökelse blant mannlige hjelpepleiere. Universitetet i Oslo, Psykologisk institutt. [*A study of male assistant nurses, University of Oslo. In Norwegian*.]

Smith, D. (1987), *The Everyday World as Problematic: A Feminist Sociology*. Milton Keynes: Open University Press.

Soini, E. (1974), *Miessairaanhoitajia kartoittava tutkimus*. Helsingin sairaanhoito-opisto. [*A study on male nurses*. School of Nursing, Helsinki. In Finnish.]

Tamminen, M. (1990), *Mies naisen maailmassa. Tutkimus päiväkotien mieslastentarhanopettajista*. Joensuun yliopisto, Kasvatustieteiden tiedekunta. [*A man in a woman's world. A study on male kindergarten teachers*. University of Joensuu. In Finnish.]

Williams, C.L. (1989), *Gender Differences at Work: Women and Men in Nontraditional Occupations*. Berkeley: University of California Press.

5 Mixed-gender Workforces: Issues in Nursing

Sarah Robinson

Nursing Research Unit, Kings College, London University

Introduction

Although men are very much a minority in the nursing profession, they have been part of its history from the outset. This chapter reviews the literature on the participation of men in nursing and identifies the main issues which have emerged. Some of these issues have been debated for many years; others are only now coming to the fore.

As Gilloran (1995) and Waddell (1995) have indicated, a review of the literature on men in nursing reveals that two topics have received most of the attention. The first concerns the entrance of men into nursing (why they enter the profession and how their backgrounds differ from those of their female counterparts); and the motivations of government departments and professional bodies to try to increase the proportion of men in the nursing workforce. The second topic focuses on the disproportionate numbers of men in management positions in nursing, and the factors which have facilitated their rise to the top of a predominantly female profession.

Much less attention has been devoted, however, to other aspects of having a mixed-gender nursing workforce. These include:

- perceptions held about male nurses by other healthcare workers;
- the nature of working relationships between male and female staff;
- the extent to which the gender of nurses is a consideration in client choice of carer;
- whether there are unmet healthcare needs which may be more appropriately addressed by male staff than by female;

- particular problems which men may encounter in the course of their work as nurses.

In this chapter, seven aspects are considered in turn; each may well have implications for other professions seeking to increase their numbers of male practitioners.

Diversity within nursing

The word 'nurse' is often used generically to refer to people who work with a diverse range of client groups. There are, however, three separate professions of nursing, midwifery and health visiting – a fact reflected in the title of the statutory body, the United Kingdom Central Council for Nursing, Midwifery and Health Visiting (UKCC). Furthermore, nursing itself is divided into four branches – adult (previously referred to as general nursing), children (previously sick children's nursing), mental health (previously mental illness nursing) and learning disability (previously mental handicap nursing). Some of the issues raised by a mixed-gender workforce are common to all branches of nursing and to midwifery and health visiting, whereas others are specific to particular areas. In this chapter reference will be made to both, but for the sake of brevity the word 'nurse' is used when discussing issues of common concern.

The proportion of men in nursing has varied over time, but has always been a minority. Figures for the hospital service showed that the proportion was 17 per cent in 1950 (MacGuire, 1969) and then fell to 14 per cent in 1959 and to 12 per cent in 1971 (Committee on Nursing, 1972). The decline over this period was due to a rise in overall recruitment, while the numbers of men remained stable (Committee on Nursing, 1972). More recently, UKCC figures for all nurses have shown a rise from 8.4 per cent men in 1990 to 9.2 per cent in 1996. However, as Table 5.1 shows, this overall figure conceals considerable variation for the different parts of the UKCC's register.

Men represent just under 6 per cent of general nurses and 2 per cent of children's nurses, but 39 per cent of psychiatric nurses. Men have only been able to enter midwifery since the 1975 Sex Discrimination Act, and numbers are still very small.

The recruitment of men

The need to increase the number of male recruits

At times of concern about staffing levels in nursing, there are usually calls to increase the numbers of men coming into the profession. For example, in the course of a detailed investigation into the education and deployment of nurses and midwives, the Briggs Committee recognized that there were shortages in all branches and recommended:

> that a concerted effort be made to recruit more male nurses in view of the potential return on investment in training and the diversity of the contribution male nurses can make to nursing. (Committee on Nursing, 1972: 171)

Men were seen as providing a better return on investment at that time, as they did not have a mid-career break for children, or indeed leave the profession altogether for family reasons.

Until the late 1980s, the nursing workforce had been characterized by a pattern of high wastage, in which those who left and did not return were replaced by a regular supply of new entrants to training, primarily female school leavers (Price Waterhouse, 1988). Warning voices sounded, however, that this reliance on school leavers could not be sustained indefinitely, as demographic changes in the population structure indicated that the mid to late 1990s would see a reduction in numbers in the younger age groups (Reid, 1986; and National Economic Development Office/ Training Agency, 1988). Therefore, the NHS was likely to be faced with a smaller pool of potential recruits on which to draw and, moreover, was likely to face increasing competition for this age group from other employers. Recommendations were made to increase the recruitment of men into the profession, and to attract mature entrants, as well as to develop strategies to facilitate the retention and return of existing staff (Reid, 1986; and National Economic Development Office/Training Agency, 1988).

The UKCC's proposals for the reform of nursing education (Project 2000) explicitly called for a 25 per cent increase in the numbers of men entering nursing each year, partly as a response to the predicted shortage of female school leavers (UKCC, 1987). As Buchan (1995) comments, it is not yet possible to establish trends relating to the gender balance from those qualifying from the new Project 2000 courses, as these have only been recorded since 1993. Early indications are that the proportion of men is greatest in mental health nursing (34 per cent), thus continuing the previous pattern, but that there may be an increase in the proportion qualifying for general nursing: 9.5 per cent of qualifiers from the adult branch are men compared with 5.9 per cent from traditional registered general nursing courses (UKCC, 1996).

Issues in recruiting men into nursing

In attempting to increase male recruitment, the nursing profession has had to consider three issues: images of nurses portrayed in recruiting material, when and how to target potential male recruits, and overcoming resistance.

Images portrayed in recruiting material

Common images and stereotypes of nurses are unlikely to attract men into the profession. Nursing has long been associated with women's work, and portrayal in the media has been primarily that of a young woman working in acute settings in a general hospital (Committee of Nursing, 1972: 78). A recruiting campaign in the late 1980s which operated under the heading 'Are you man enough to do women's work?' was felt in retrospect to have been unsuccessful, as it had the reverse of the intended effect by associating nursing exclusively with women (Holloway, 1992). There has been much discussion about suitable images to attract men, for example, focusing on high-technology aspects of nursing (Cottingham, 1987). The most recent Department of Health campaign, aimed at both men and women, has not used pictures of nurses but has focused on real-life incidents, each underpinned with the challenge 'Nursing – have you got what it takes?' Regardless of the images of nursing portrayed in advertisements, the profession has to contend with a current public perception of nursing as entailing long hours, staff shortages and low pay (Cole, 1994). Pay in particular has long been regarded as deterring men from entering nursing (Gaze, 1987). Moreover, research suggests that advertisements in the national media may not be the most effective means of targeting potential recruits, in that the majority of registered general nurses taking part in a longitudinal study of their careers reported that by the time they saw advertisements they had already decided to take nurse training (Murrells, Robinson and Marsland, 1995).

Timing of recruitment campaigns
Decisions about how and when to target potential male recruits is more difficult than decisions for targeting female recruits. Women tend to make the decision to take nurse training in their mid-teens, often having wanted to nurse from an early age (MacGuire, 1969; Soothill, Bradby and Williams, 1994; and Marsland, Robinson and Murrells, 1995). Thus, nursing as a career can be brought to their attention while at school or sixth form college. Deciding how best to target men is more difficult. Many studies have shown that men are older than women on entering nursing and that it is much less likely to have been their first choice of occupation (MacGuire, 1969; Brown and Stones, 1973; Hardy, 1987a; Skevington and Dawkes, 1988; Soothill Bradby and Williams, 1994; and Marsland, Robinson and Murrells, 1995). At the time when they do decide to enter nursing, they are likely to be in a much more diverse range of educational and employment settings than women and so recruiting material requires wider distribution.

Overcoming resistance to becoming a nurse
A number of studies have shown that boys are less likely than girls to have nursing brought to their attention as a possible career while at school, and, if they do express an interest, they are more likely than girls to be discouraged from this course of action by school teachers, friends and parents, especially fathers (Hardy, 1987a; and Murrells, Robinson and Marsland, 1995).

The over-representation of men in senior posts

The effect of the recommendations of the Salmon Report

Considerable interest has focused on the extent to which men hold a disproportionate number of the top posts in nursing. The turning point for men's rapid advancement up the career ladder is usually regarded as the implementation of the Salmon Report's recommendations for a line management system in nursing (Ministry of Health, 1966). Prior to this, men's career prospects had been restricted in several ways (Dingwall, 1979; Castledine, 1994; and Dolan, 1993). For example, general nursing training for men had been restricted to certain hospitals and, until 1949, men's names were held on a separate register. In psychiatric nursing (the area in which most male nurses worked), women who held a general and a psychiatric nursing qualification were brought in as matrons to raise the status of psychiatric nursing. Furthermore, men were not admitted to membership of the Royal College of Nursing until 1960. The reasons for this relegation of men have been much discussed; but the view that it ensured female dominance in one of the few areas of work open to middle-class women is the one cited most often (Dolan, 1993).

At the time that Salmon was conducting his enquiries, the majority of the top posts were held by women: figures included in the report show that in England and Wales there were 1,835 matrons and 210 male chief nurses, and that figures for Scotland were 284 and 14 respectively (Ministry of Health, 1966). At this time, there were no posts between a departmental charge nurse/ward sister and the matron/chief male nurse (or their deputies). Salmon recommended a hierarchy of posts from charge nurse/ward sister through nursing officers, senior nursing officers, principal nursing officers to chief nursing officers. The introduction of this line management system into nursing was seen by Carpenter (1977) as a critique of female authority; the Salmon Report suggested that when women move from being ward nurses to administrators 'they seem unable to make decisions' (Ministry of Health, 1966). Female nurses were seen as being indecisive, paying too much attention to detail, and being less able to stand the strain of life at the top (Davies and Conn, 1993).

Soon after the new hierarchy was in place, figures appeared which indicated the extent to which men were climbing the new managerial ladder. Dingwall's (1972) analysis of Scottish figures, for example, showed that the proportion of men in general nursing posts above ward charge nurses trebled between 1964 and 1969, while surveys conducted for the Briggs report showed that approximately one-third of the two top grades in the Salmon hierarchy of posts were held by male nurses (Committee on Nursing, 1972). An investigation into the role of the nursing officer showed that men held 30 per cent of these posts, and 48 per cent of district nursing officer posts (Jones, Crossley-Holland and Matus, 1981). This study also showed that this disproportionate representation was evident in all branches of nursing. Thus, in psychiatric nursing, where men represented just over one-third of the workforce, they held 71 per cent of nursing officer posts (Jones, Crossley-Holland and Matus, 1981). Nuttall's examination of the 1982 figures for England showed that men held 44 per cent of the district nursing officer posts and 51 per cent of the directors of nursing education posts, despite the fact that in the period during which these postholders would have qualified, the percentage of men never exceeded 6 per cent of those qualifying as registered general nurses (Nuttall, 1983). A 1985 study of chief nursing officers found that 46 per cent were male (Hutt, 1985).

The Salmon nursing hierarchy was the subject of much criticism in the Griffiths report on NHS management (Department of Health and Social Services, 1983) and some of the posts in the hierarchy were lost with the introduction of general management into the health service. These posts were open to non-nurses – as Gaze (1987) reports – however, the over-representation of men persisted. Thus, of the 622 unit general managers appointed by 1987, 71 were nurses; however, less than half (33) were women. The trend has continued to be in evidence in reports published in the 1990s. A 1992 study, for example, found that men were almost three times as likely as women to be in a senior nursing position (Seccombe and Ball, 1992). A more recent study showed that women were better represented in senior nursing posts than hitherto, but that male nurses still did proportionally better in securing general management positions (IHSM Consultants, 1995).

It is not only in nursing management and education that men are over-represented; the same trend has emerged to some extent in professional and statutory bodies. Nuttall (1983) observed that 'any meeting of nurses, whether the Royal College of Nursing (RCN) or The Confederation of Health Service Employees (COHSE) will demonstrate that it is the men who are more vocal and who hold office.' That this trend occurs early on in nursing careers is reflected in Mill's observation about the Association of Nursing students: 'when it comes to elections, it tends to be the men who are prepared to fight' (Mills, rep. in Gaze, 1987). Although the top positions in the UKCC and Royal College of Nursing are currently held by women, both have been held by men in the past. Perhaps the only top position in nursing not to have been held by a man as yet is that of Chief Nursing Officer at the Department of Health.

Turning briefly to the midwifery profession, men have only been able to train as midwives since the 1975 Sex Discrimination Act. An early study indicated that they do not appear to want to move out of clinical practice to the same extent as their counterparts in nursing (Lewis, 1991). At present, just one of the 100 heads of the midwifery service is a man, and, similarly, one of the 80 directors of midwifery education (Lewis, personal communication), although Edwards (1994) reports that men are now over-represented among middle managers and teachers.

Factors contributing to the career progress of men

Alongside the mounting evidence that men were 'taking over the profession' (Nuttall, 1983), various studies were undertaken to explore the processes which had enabled men to be so much more successful than women in obtaining senior posts. Particularly illuminating are studies of men and women in top positions in nursing (Hardy, 1987a and 1987b; and Hutt, 1985), and studies of career patterns of staff in two health districts (Davies and Rosser, 1986), in two mental health units (Hunt, 1991) and in three health districts (Winson, 1992). The following picture emerged from these studies.

In nursing, as in other professions, career progress was faster for those who did not take breaks. The majority of pre-Salmon matrons were single women (84 per cent of those in England and Wales, 92 per cent of those in Scotland); they devoted their lives to the service, often living in the hospital. Although the proportion of married women in nursing subsequently increased, the career model likely to lead to promotion remained that of the single woman with no breaks in service. The familiar pattern of breaks for childcare followed by a return to a part-time post which was often at a lower grade, meant that women were disadvantaged in comparison with men. Hutt's and Hardy's research both showed that women with top posts were far more likely to be single than men in comparable posts. Other family factors were also relevant. Married men were more likely than married women to be able to make the geographical moves necessary for career progress, given the prevailing ethos of family moves to facilitate a man's career but not a woman's. Married nurses in dual-earner households were disadvantaged in that their income was much more likely to be the lower of the two and, therefore, seen as expendable. Dependent elderly relatives also emerged as a restriction on women's mobility, but not on that of men's.

Within the profession, men were more likely than women to have mentors who helped them in planning career moves (Winson, 1992). Although men gained fewer qualifications than women after registration, those that they did have were more likely to impress promotion panels (Hardy, 1987a and 1987b). Davies and Rosser (1986) also found that some female nurses stood back to allow men to go forward for promotion, on the grounds that they were the breadwinners, whereas they regarded their own wage as the supplementary part of the family income.

Future trends in men obtaining senior posts

Is this pattern of the over-representation of male nurses in senior posts likely to continue? Research shows that men qualifying from traditional courses are still more likely than women to do so with the intention of seeking a post in management. For example, Marsland, Robinson and Murrells (1995) found that of 1,015 registered general nurses qualifying in 1990–1991, 29 per cent of men compared with 11 per cent of women planned to seek a post in management, and Robinson et al. (1996) found that of 447 registered mental nurses qualifying in 1993–1994, 42 per cent of men compared with 28 per cent of women planned to do so. However, the NHS in which they find themselves offers very different career structures from those of the Salmon era. Management structures have been flattened and the emphasis is much more on lateral career paths and developing advanced and specialist roles in clinical practice (Department of Health, 1995). Some commentators have observed that men in particular may find difficulties in adapting to the new career environment (Beard, ref. in Naish, 1996). On the other hand, while various policy initiatives to advance the careers of women have been introduced into the NHS at local and national levels, these do not as yet represent a coherent and sustained strategy (Davies and Conn, 1993; and Davies, 1995).

Perceptions held about male nurses

A small volume of literature focuses on perceptions held about male nurses by other healthcare professionals, in particular female nurses. This consists of articles written by male nurses and a few small-scale research studies. Three themes emerge most frequently: assumptions about sexual orientation; ability to 'care' and interest in promotion.

Assumptions about sexual orientation
Men working in areas in which they are very much in the minority – general and children's nursing, and midwifery – report encountering a widespread assumption on the part of female nurses and medical staff, as well as the general public, that they are homosexual (Levine, 1983; Wilcox, 1987; Haywood, 1994; Seed, 1995; Waddell, 1995). To a lesser extent, it has been reported that men encounter the view that they have joined a female-dominated profession as a means of increasing the likelihood of having relationships with women (Seed, 1995).

Ability to care
Male nurses may be regarded by their female colleagues as not possessing the qualities which the latter see as being the essence of providing

patient care. This was indicated in a study by Choon and Skevington (1984) in which 92 psychiatric nurses (21 men and 71 women) were asked to complete a Burns Semantic Differential Questionnaire to indicate the characteristics which they perceived themselves (as either male or female nurses) as possessing and the characteristics which they perceived the other group as possessing. The main findings were that the male nurses saw both male and female nurses as possessing those nursing qualities popularly stereotyped as 'feminine' – being kind, warm and affectionate – whereas the female nurses saw themselves, but not the male nurses, as possessing these characteristics. Certainly, several male nurses in writing of their experiences, describe encountering the view from female colleagues that men cannot 'care' in the way in which women can (e.g. Castledine, 1994; and Harding, 1994). These men contest the assumption that caring is a female specific attribute. Harding (1994), for example, argues that 'to believe that women have a natural vocational monopoly on caring is both simplistic and naive'.

Interest in promotion
As shown above, men are more likely than women to obtain promotion. Many men do, however, remain in clinical practice and some have written that this is where they see their career as being based. A charge nurse of ten years' standing writes: 'I find that I have a very important role to play in clinical practice and I have chosen to stay' (Charles, ref. in Naish, 1996).

The fact that men do hold a disproportionate number of senior posts may colour female nurses' perceptions of all male nurses. For example, in a study of nurses' perceptions of their work and conditions, Mackay (1989) found that half the respondents said male nurses were more career minded than female nurses. From a study of male and female nurses working in an intensive care unit, Porter (1992) reports that the women invariably regarded the men as being 'on their way to higher things'. Male nurses have also reported that whereas all their female colleagues may regard them as progressing towards promotion, their responses to this may vary. Some female nurses express resentment (Porter, 1992; and

Waddell, 1995), whereas others think less well of those men who choose not to leave clinical practice (Charles, ref. in Naish, 1996).

Working relationships

As Gilloran (1995) comments, very little research exists on how male and female nurses perceive their working relationships. Several aspects of these, however, have been written about by male nurses, or explored in small-scale research projects, including being singled out, being expected to undertake certain tasks, perceptions of who does what, and relating to medical staff.

Being singled out
Although perhaps a minor point, male nurses have described with some irritation the way in which female nurses invariably refer to them as *male* nurses, whereas they themselves would prefer to be described simply as nurses (Swaffeld, 1988; Goad, 1992; Haywood, 1994; and Waddell, 1995). Goad (1992), for example, when describing his community experience, reported that the district nurse to whom he was allocated always introduced him to clients by saying, 'This is Nick, he's the male student nurse.'

Special identification is also reflected in the way in which male nurses are treated by female staff, particularly when they are students. They tend to be viewed as one of two extremes – either dreadful or, more often, as 'wonderful'. Tagg (1981), for example, in a study of responses to male and female students on postnatal wards reported that the latter felt neglected by the ward staff. Staff and students reported that attention focused on ensuring that the male student obtained all the necessary experience and he was seen as the 'blue-eyed boy who could do no wrong' (Tagg, 1981). Davies and Rosser (1986) found in their study of nurses' career patterns that the men were seen 'primarily as men and secondarily as nurses' and were picked out as 'wonderful'. The persistence of this attitude was indicated in a more recent study by Walby and Greenwell (1994). Comments made during interviews held with nurses in five hospitals suggested that male nurses were seen as 'treasured outsiders' – for example 'As students, males get the cushiest of jobs, get let off early, have extended breaks' and 'Pampered by other nurses'.

Expectations to undertake certain tasks

A source of resentment for male nurses is the expectation that they should undertake certain tasks. Those cited include being a handy man on the ward. Oaker (ref. in Swaffield, 1988) for example, describes being greeted by a ward sister with the words, 'Oh, you're a man – these shelves need fixing.' Other male commentators have described how in general nursing, it is sometimes expected that men should lift heavy patients, but point out that safe lifting requires technique, not strength. In psychiatric nursing, male students have reported that they have been expected to be involved in patient restraint, simply because they were men, although having little or no experience in the use of appropriate techniques (McCarthy ref. in Swaffield, 1988). This emerged as a major concern for male nursing students in a longitudinal study of the experiences of 36 psychiatric nurse learners (Robinson, 1991).

Perceptions of division of responsibility

In response to the lack of research about working relations between male and female nurses, Gilloran (1995) undertook an interview study with 15 staff (ten women and five men) working in three of the psychogeriatric wards in a Scottish hospital. The female nurses believed that they shouldered more of the burden of the routine work, for example noticing that incontinent patients needed a change of underwear. They also believed that women paid greater attention to the details of basic nursing care; a particular example given was that if something was spilt on a patient's clothes, a female nurse would change the garment whereas a male nurse would just give it a wipe. When male staff were asked about differences in care delivery, they said that men were more confident in managerial roles and in decision making, whereas women were 'better at the feeling things, like intuition and warmth' (Gilloran, 1995).

Relating to medical staff

Although this chapter focuses on differences between the experiences of male and female nurses, it is important in any discussion of nursing to recognize that the major 'gender' issue is the relationship between the mainly female profession of nursing and the male-dominated profession of medicine. As Davies (1995) has recently documented, a considerable volume of scholarship exists exploring gender and nursing, much of which focuses on the nature of nurse–doctor interactions. Of relevance to this chapter, however, is whether male nurses are more assertive than female nurses in their working relationships with doctors. Studies undertaken to date suggest that greater assertiveness is unlikely. Such a conclusion was reached by Porter (1992) for example, from observing interactions between 33 nurses (30 women and three men) and 21 doctors (six women and 15 men) in an intensive care unit during a three-month period in 1989. By recording the number of times male and female nurses made evaluative comments to doctors in reply to medical requests, Porter showed that the gender of nurses appeared to have little effect on the nature of their interaction with medical staff. A similar conclusion was drawn by Walby et al. (1994) from a 1990–1991 study of 127 doctors (97 men and 30 women) and 135 nurses (19 men and 116 women) working in hospitals selected from across the UK. As with Porter's study, the nursing staff included both staff nurses and charge nurse/ward sister and the medical staff included all grades from senior house officer to consultant. For each of a series of potentially conflict related issues between medical and nursing staff, no significant differences were found between male and female nurses as to whether they would report the conflict and this remained whether the doctor was male or female. Porter (1992) and Walby et al. (1994) suggest that their findings support the thesis of the structural determination of gender relations and occupations rather than socialization theories. As Porter (1992) puts it, 'the inability of male nurses to use the advantages of their gender is the result of the ascription to nursing of a position of female subordination.'

Preferences for gender of carer

Assumptions about preferences

The participation of men in the nursing workforce has raised the issue of patient preferences for the gender of nurses providing their care. Much of the existing research on preferences for gender of healthcare worker has focused on whether women users of primary healthcare services prefer female general practitioners (see Brooks and Phillips, 1996, for a review). Little research has focused on patients' preferences for the gender of their nurse. The subject has, however, been a particular bone of contention for male nursing students. Looking back at their nursing education, men have reported that they were not allowed placements in gynaecology or in female medical or surgical wards (e.g. Oaker, ref. in Swaffield, 1988), and on mixed-sex wards they were allocated to male patients only. In contrast, women students were allocated to care for both male and female patients. By 1988, complaints about experiences of the kinds described above were sufficient for the Association of Nursing Students to propose a motion at that year's Royal College of Nursing Congress that Council investigate 'the widespread inequalities in nursing training, based on gender'. However, reports of similar experiences have continued to appear throughout the 1990s (e.g. Goad, 1992; Haywood, 1994; Castledine, 1994; and Waddell, 1995).

Men have challenged these practices on two grounds. First, whereas it is assumed that women might object to being nursed by a man, there is no recognition that men might equally object to intimate procedures being carried out by female nurses (Castledine, 1994; and Haywood, 1994). As Castledine (1994) comments, when a male nurse appears on a female ward, privacy suddenly becomes an important issue, and yet this is often not even considered when female nurses work on male wards. Second, men have argued that patients should always have the choice over the gender of the nurse looking after them, particularly if intimate procedures are to be carried out or they want to discuss sexual or emotional problems (Haywood, 1994; and Waddell, 1995).

Research into patient preferences

Little is known about patient preferences for the gender of nurses allocated to their care. Cahoon (1978) identified it as a subject which urgently needed exploring, yet Gilloran (1995) writing 17 years later, found that it was still much under-researched. Studies which have been undertaken have focused mainly on women patients' views about receiving care from male staff (e.g. Tagg, 1981; and Lodge et al., 1997), although others have focused on both sexes (e.g. Mathieson, 1991).

In Tagg's study the reactions of women on postnatal wards to being cared for by male students were the subject of a questionnaire survey (Tagg, 1981). Of those women who had received care from a male student (34), 100 per cent said that they enjoyed being looked after by him, and 76 per cent had felt able to confide in him about their own or their baby's needs. Occasional embarrassment was reported over assistance with personal hygiene and using bedpans. Women's views about being nursed by a man were explored by Lodge et al. (1997) in a study undertaken on a gynaecological oncology ward. Women were asked to complete a questionnaire in which they rated the level of embarrassment they felt in relation to a range of procedures being carried out by a male rather than a female nurse. The main finding to emerge was that women only preferred female nurses if they had never been admitted to hospital before.

Preferences for the gender of nurses providing care emerged from a study of psychiatric patients undertaken by Mathieson (1991). Semi-structured interviews were held with 52 of the 76 patients on the acute wards of a Scottish psychiatric hospital. Twenty-five of the participants were women and 27 were men, within an age range of 17–90. Most were informally detained and had a wide range of psychiatric problems, but the author reports that all were able to make perceptive and pertinent comments. All had experience of being cared for by both female and male nurses. Twenty-two of the 25 women said that they preferred female nurses, and objections to care from male nurses were voiced in relation to bed bathing (17), being assisted to the toilet (13) and discussing sexual (13) and physical problems (six). Men were less likely to express a preference, with only eight of the 27 preferring to be nursed by a man. Ten, however, said that they were unwilling to discuss sexual problems with a female nurse.

The studies reported here indicate that patients may well have preferences for the gender of nurses providing their care, albeit that for some client groups these patients are a minority. As Mathieson (1991) observes, patient preferences in this respect have implications for decisions about staffing levels and staff gender mix, and for individual nurses in ensuring that patients' feelings are ascertained and respected. It is also important not to assume that patients are unable to make a choice, particularly those who are seriously ill (mentally or physically), elderly or have learning disabilities.

Developing new areas of care

A benefit of having men working in traditionally female professions has been the opportunity to meet previously unaddressed health needs. Health visiting provides an interesting case in point. Traditionally associated with the care of women and young children, health visitors are now expected to meet the healthcare needs of all groups of the population (UKCC, 1988). The promotion of men's health has received far less attention than the promotion of women's health (Fareed, 1994) and, influenced by the development of well-woman clinics, some male health visitors have tried to address this problem by setting up well-man clinics (Deans, 1988; and Brown and Lunt, 1992). These focused primarily on advising men about diet, smoking and exercise, but also on HIV, testicular cancer, family planning and stress. It has also been suggested that male health visitors could develop an important role in discussing contraception with men from ethnic minority groups, who may be unwilling to have such discussions with women (Barton, 1990). In relation to midwifery, Lewis's male respondents said that they felt that their presence gave the women's partners moral support, and enabled them to participate more fully in the care of their partner (Lewis, 1991).

Areas of concern for male nurses

In recent years, two aspects of professional life have emerged of particular concern to men: abuse of children in the care of nurses and the disproportionate number of men appearing before the UKCC Professional Conduct Committee.

Nurses are involved in the care of children in a variety of settings. These include children who are inpatients in hospital, children brought to accident and emergency departments and to general practitioner surgeries, children attending child psychiatry services, children who live in, or attend, centres for those with learning disabilities, and children who are visited at home. In recent years, the profession has had to consider the risks of children being harmed by nurses and the risk of false allegations being made against staff. This has been occasioned by an increased awareness of potential problems in the wake of isolated but high-profile cases in which nurses have been convicted of harming children. The dilemma, as Glasper and Campbell (1994) observe, is one of how to keep a sense of proportion – so that the natural human act of hugging a distressed child is not open to misinterpretation. These two authors, both children's nurses, posed the following questions for nursing.

- Should professional bodies provide guidelines for male nurses working with children?
- Should personality testing be mandatory for those working with children?
- Should male nurses be chaperoned when carrying out intimate procedures on children?

In 1996, the Royal College of Nursing issued guidelines for good practice which were designed to protect children from harm and nurses from false allegations. Although the guidelines were addressed to all staff, it was acknowledged that men might be more likely than women to find themselves in vulnerable situations (Royal College of Nursing, 1996).

Although men represent only 9 per cent of the profession, they appear in 44 per cent of the cases brought before the UKCC's Professional Conduct Committee (UKCC, 1996). The type of offence occurring most often is the expression of physical or verbal aggression towards patients. These figures have occasioned considerable concern and a variety of explanations have been offered (Cole, 1993). In 1995, Tariq Hussein, the assistant registrar at the UKCC, stressed that 'there is a need to see whether we properly prepare nurses, and particularly men, for situations where the power relationship is one in which they have predominance' (Cohen, 1995).

Conclusions

The early history of male nurses was very much one of being seen as 'second-class citizens'. In reviewing the volume of more recent comment and research, male nurses could perhaps conclude that there is still a somewhat ambivalent attitude to their participation in the profession. Whenever a recruitment crisis looms, there is a call to recruit more men (e.g. Committee on Nursing, 1972; and UKCC, 1986). Once members of the profession, however, they might well feel that they are 'tarred with the brush' of only being interested in promotion and, once in a senior post, perpetuating a system which has discriminated against their female colleagues. While often singled out as special and perhaps receiving preferential treatment, particularly as students, they may nonetheless encounter a range of assumptions about the role which they should play in the delivery of care. Although the belief was expressed that increasing the number of men in nursing would lead to higher status and pay (Gaze, 1987), they have subsequently been castigated in some quarters for the failure of these objectives to materialize (News item, *Nursing Standard*, 1994: 52).

There has been much less consideration of the contribution which men make to the profession and of distinctive areas of practice which they may be well placed to develop. Castledine (1994) comments that there have been few references to 'men in nursing and their contribution has received only slight mention in nursing history books'. In looking to the future, hopes have been expressed that the generation of nurses now qualifying from the new diploma courses will be less bound by the stereotypes of the past, and that the health service they enter may afford equal recognition to the role of men and women both in clinical practice and in management (Dolan, 1993).

It could be argued that some of the issues which have emerged from this consideration of having a mixed-gender workforce in nursing have implications for other professions seeking to increase their number of male practitioners. These include overcoming the image of the work as being the sole preserve of women and developing recruitment strategies to enhance the likelihood of its consideration by men. Enabling clients to discuss their preferences for the gender of their carers is important, as is not making *a priori* assumptions about what these preferences might be. An open and constructive attitude to the discussion of working relationships between male and female staff may serve to lessen the likelihood of resentment about who should, or who is, taking responsibility for particular aspects of the work. Finally, an issue relevant to all occupations and not only those involved in healthcare, is the implementation of employment practices which provide both women and men with equal opportunities for promotion and career development.

Acknowledgements

I should like to record my thanks to Louise Marsland, with whom I have discussed many of the topics in this chapter and for her comments on a draft, and to Rachel Hardyman for help with the literature search.

References

Barton, A. (1990), 'The problems facing men as health visitors', *Nursing Standard*, 28(4), 28.

Brooks, F. and Phillips, D. (1996), ' Do women want women health workers? Women's views of the primary healthcare service', *Journal of Advanced Nursing*, 23(6), 1207–1211.

Brown, I. and Lunt, F. (1992), 'Evaluating a well-man clinic', *Health Visitor*, 65(1), 12–14.

Brown, R.G. and Stones, R.W. (1973), *The Male Nurse. Occasional Papers on Social Administration*, 52. London: G Bell & Sons.

Buchan, J. (1995), 'Male nurses: losing their job advantage', *Nursing Standard*, *10*(9), 30.

Cahoon, M.C. (1978) 'The male-female dichotomy in the nursing profession in a time of social change: more male nurses but increasing numbers of female patients – an international perspective? *Journal of Advanced Nursing*, *3*, 65–72.

Carpenter, M. (1977), 'The new managerialism and professionalism in nursing'. In: M. Stacey, M. Reid, C. Heath and R. Dingwall (eds), *Health and the Division of Labour*. London: Croom Helm.

Castledine, G. (1994), 'Men in nursing: in remembrance of Trevor Clay', *British Journal of Nursing*, *3*(9), 467–468.

Choon, G.L. and Skevington, S.M. (1984), 'How do women and men in nursing perceive each other?'. In: S.M. Skevington (ed.), *Understanding Nurses: the Social Psychology of Nursing*. Chichester: John Wiley.

Cohen, P. (1995), 'Men behaving badly', *Nursing Times*, *91*(45), 18.

Cole, A. (1993), 'Men and misconduct', *Nursing Times*, *89*(46), 10.

— (1994), 'Future imperfect', *Nursing Times*, *90*(39), 14–15.

Committee on Nursing (1972), *Report of the Committee on Nursing*. (Chairman: Professor Asa Briggs). London: HMSO.

Cottingham, M. (1987), 'Are you man enough to do women's work? *Nursing Times*, *83*(20), 28–29.

Davies, C. (1995), *Gender and the Professional Predicament in Nursing*. Buckingham: Open University Press.

— and Conn, L. (1993), *Creating Compatible Careers: A Report and a Selected Bibliography on Career Paths in Nursing*. London: National Health Service Executive.

— and Rosser, J. (1986), *Processes of Discrimination: A Report on a Study of Women Working in the NHS*. London: DHSS.

Deans, W. (1988), 'Well man clinics', *Nursing*, *3*(26), 975–978.

Department of Health (1995), *Career Pathways – Nursing, Midwifery and Health Visiting*. London: Department of Health.

Department of Health and Social Security (1983), *NHS Management Inquiry (Griffiths Report)*. London: DHSS.

Dingwall, R. (1972), 'Nursing: towards a male-dominated occupation?', *Nursing Times*, October 12.

— (1979), 'The place of men in nursing'. In: M. Colledge and D. Jones (eds), *Readings in Nursing*. Churchill Livingstone.

Dolan, B. (1993), 'Gender and change'. In: B. Dolan (ed.), *Project 2000: Reflection and Celebration*. London: Scutari Press.

Edwards, G. (1994), 'Jobs for the boys: male domination within nursing and midwifery', *British Journal of Midwifery*, *2*(10), 504–506.

Fareed, A. (1994), 'Equal rights for men', *Nursing Times*, *90*(5), 26–29.

Gaze, H. (1987), 'Man appeal', *Nursing Times*, 5(20), 24–27.

Gilloran, A. (1995), 'Gender differences in care delivery and supervisory relationship: the case of psychogeriatric nursing', *Journal of Advanced Nursing*, *21*(4), 652–658.

Glasper, E. and Campbell, S. (1994), 'Beyond the Clothier Inquiry', *Nursing Standard*, *8*(28),18–19.

Goad, N. (1992), 'Second class male?', *Nursing Standard*, *6*(30), 53.

Harding, I. (1994), 'Gender gap', *Nursing Standard*, *8*(39), 39.

Hardy, L. (1987a), 'The male model', *Nursing Times*, *83*(21), 36–38.

— (1987b), 'Unequal opportunity', *Nursing Times*, *83*(22), 45–47.

Haywood, M. (1994), 'Male order', *Nursing Times*, *89*(20), 52.

Holloway, J. (1992), 'The media representation of the nurse: the implications for nursing'. In: K. Soothill, C. Henry and K. Kendrick (eds), *Themes and Perspectives in Nursing*. London: Chapman and Hall.

Hunt, M. (1991), 'Who flies highest?', *Nursing Times*, *87*(7), 29–31.

Hutt, R. (1985), *Chief Officer Career Profiles: A Study of the Backgrounds, Training and Career Experiences of Regional and District Nursing Officers*. Brighton: Institute of Manpower Studies, University of Sussex.

IHSM Consultants (1995), *Creative Career Paths in the NHS Report No. 4: Senior Nurses*. A Study by IHSM Consultants for the NHS Women's Unit. London: Department of Health.

Jones, D., Crossley-Holland, C. and Matus, T. (1981), *The Role of the Nursing Officer*. London: Department of Health and Social Security.

Levine, I. (1983), 'Machismo and the male nurse', *Nursing Times*, *79*(21), 50–51.

Lewis, P. (1991), 'Men in midwifery: their experiences as students and as practitioners'. In: S. Robinson and A. Thomson (eds), *Midwives, Research and Childbirth: Volume 2*. London: Chapman and Hall.

MacGuire, J. (1969), 'Threshold to nursing', *Occasional Papers on Social Administration no. 38*. London: London School of Economics.

MacGuire, J. (1980), 'Nursing'. In R. Silverstone and A. Ward (eds) *Careers of Professional Women*. London: Croom Helm.

Mackay, L. (1989), *Nursing a Problem*. Buckingham: Open University Press.

Marsland, L., Robinson, S. and Murrells, T. (1996), 'Pursuing a career in nursing: differences between men and women qualifying as registered general nurses', *Journal of Nursing Management*, *4*(4), 231–241.

Mathieson, E. (1991), 'A question of gender', *Nursing Times*, *87*(7), 31–32.

Ministry of Health, Scottish Home and Health Department (1966), *Report of the Committee on Senior Nursing Staff Structure*. Chairman: B. Salmon. London: HMSO.

Murrells, T., Robinson, S. and Marsland, L. (1995), ' Deciding to pursue nurse education: sources of information, influence and encouragement', *Nurse Education Today*, *15*(6), 397–405.

Naish, J. (1996), 'Men's talk', *Nursing Times*, *92*(26), 30–31.

National Economic Development Office/Training Agency (1988), *Young People and the Labour Market*. London: NEDO/Training Agency.

Nuttall, P. (1983), 'Male takeover or female giveaway?', *Nursing Times*, *1*(12), 10–11.

Porter, S. (1992), 'Women in a women's job: the gendered experience of nurses', *Sociology of Health and Illness*, *14*(4), 510–527.

Price Waterhouse (1988), *Nurse Retention and Recruitment: A matter of priority*. Bristol: Price Waterhouse.

Reid, N.G. (1986), 'Nurse manpower: the problems ahead', *International Journal of Nursing Studies*, *23*(3), 187–197.

Robinson, S. (1991), *Learning About Violence: Educational Opportunities for Learner Nurses*. Report to the Department of Health, Nursing Research Unit, King's College, University of London.

—, Kipping, C., Hickey, G. and Murrells, T. (1996), *Getting Started: Phase of a Study of Psychiatric Nurses' Careers*. Report to Department of Health, Nursing Research Unit, King's College, London University.

Royal College of Nursing (1996), *Protection of Nurses Working with Children and Young People; Issues in Nursing and Health (NPC/2/96)*. London: Royal College of Nursing.

Seccombe, I. and Ball, I.J. (1992), *Motivation, Morale and Mobility. A Profile of Qualified Nurses in the 1990s*. Institute of Manpower Studies, University of Sussex, Brighton.

Seed, A. (1995), 'Crossing the boundaries – experiences of neophyte nurses', *Journal of Advanced Nursing*, *21*, 1136–1143.

Skevington, S. and Dawkes, D. (1988), 'Fred Nightingale', *Nursing Times*, *84*(21), 49–51.

Soothill, K., Bradby, M. and Williams, C. (1994), 'Demographic details and family background of nursing recruits', *British Journal of Nursing*, *3*(8), 397–402.

Swaffield, L. (1988), 'Stand by your man', *Nursing Times*, *84*(20), 68.

Tagg, P. (1981), 'Male nurses in midwifery', *Nursing Times*, *77*(43), 1851–1853.

UKCC (1987), *Project 2000 – The Final Proposals*. London: UKCC.

— (1988), *Health Visiting Requirement for Obstetric Experience*. London: UKCC.

— (1996) *Statistical Analysis of the Council's Professional Register – April 1995 to March 1996*. London: UKCC.

Waddell, K. (1995), 'Nursing a gender', *Nursing Standard*, *9*(30), 62.

Walby, S. and Greenwell, S., with Mackay, L. and Soothill, K. (1994), *Medicine and Nursing: Professions in a Changing Health Service*. London: Sage Publications.

Wilcox, G. (1987), 'Male models', *Nursing Times*, *83*(12), 70.

Winson, G. (1992), 'A study of nurse career paths', *Senior Nurse*, *12*(3), 11–19.

6 Men Working with Young Children: A *Natural* Development?

Sue Smedley
Roehampton Institute, London

Introduction

Discussions at the seminar suggested that there was some agreement with the widely held assumption that there is a need for more men to work with young children. However, if we don't ask why more men are needed, the discussion might remain based on unquestioned assumptions and little will be achieved. Many different reasons can be put forward to support the recruitment of men into childcare services. One such argument which can take on the status of being beyond question relates to what is perceived as natural. The following two statements emerged in discussions at the seminar:

- it is natural to have a balance in the numbers of men and women in the workplace;
- it is natural for children to be cared for by men as well as by women.

The notion of what is 'natural' is also (perhaps an unexplored) part of the different expectations that can be made of girls and boys. This chapter sets out some of the problems associated with the notion of what is 'natural' and raises some questions about an underlying concept: the masculine/feminine dichotomy.[1]

What is described as natural can seem to be common sense. It can become an unnoticed and unquestioned part of the culture. For that very reason, we should pause to consider it more deeply to increase awareness and understanding of the contexts of discussions about men working with young children. What are the consequences of drawing on the discourse of the natural in discussions about gender and work with young children? What is natural is not straightforward; what is taken to be the 'natural order of things' is a socially constructed concept. What is natural (and what is assumed to be traditional) is continually negotiated and constructed by individuals in social and cultural contexts, where power relations play a significant part. 'There can be no truth which stands outside the condition of its own production' (Walkerdine, 1985: 238).

What is natural?

Raymond Williams describes 'nature' as 'perhaps the most complex word in the language' (Williams, 1983: 219) and traces the different ways the word has been used, some of which seem to be echoed in current discussions about men working with young children.

In the eighteenth and nineteenth centuries conceptions of nature were based on beliefs in the existence of natural laws, which could fuel arguments for social change or reform. What was natural was seen as linked with 'goodness and innocence' (Williams, 1983: 223) and had an inherent validity. Nature was set in opposition to that which had been created by human beings. Therefore, natural laws and the arguments based on them can seem to have an unquestionable status. The concept of what is natural must, however, be questioned and explored in discussions about men working with young children.

There are many contradictions in the midst of arguments that centre on what is natural. Working with young children is assumed to be 'naturally' women's work. It is seen as an extension of motherhood and, therefore, appropriate work for women. Historically, work with young children (either as a governess or as an elementary teacher) was thought to be one of few occupations suitable for women, drawing on women's 'innate nature' (Vicinus, 1985: 15). Miller (1996), Steedman (1985) and Walkerdine (1983) have shown these assumptions to be problematic.

At the same time, it might be argued that it is not natural for young children, especially boys, to be cared for only by women. This viewpoint has a history, as Oram (1987) explains. In the 1920s and 1930s the

National Association of Schoolmasters claimed that men were needed to teach boys. 'Although the different roles of men and women in society were assumed to be "natural", the manly instinct had to be taught, a contradiction frequently expressed by the NAS [National Association of Schoolmasters]' (Oram, 1987: 102). Hockenjos laments the low numbers of men in the caring services and asks how boys will learn to care if they have no access to male role models. 'In the absence of a more balanced workforce,' he argues, it may seem to children as if 'only women have got what it takes' (Hockenjos, 1996: 2). Here, arguments about what is natural are joined by notions of balance. Similar arguments are put forward in the primary school context, 'Pupils need a balance of experience from different teachers. Having men and women provides that balance' (Cook, ref. in Wallace, 1995). However, there are questions that should be asked here. Do men offer something different in their work with young children on account of their being men? Is there an underlying assumption that boys can only learn gender appropriately from men? What versions of masculinity and femininity are behind such arguments? Is the category 'men' assumed to be homogeneous?

In contrast, some might argue that it is unnatural for men to work with young children. 'In a stereotyped world, if working with young children is a "natural" occupation for women, men who want to work with them must be "unnatural"' (Aspinwall and Drummond, 1989: 15). Men are making a non-traditional choice if they work in childcare services and that can be read as an unnatural choice. This is based on particular versions of what it means to be a man: to be part of a public, professional world of work, rather than involved in a workplace perceived as semi-domesticated and feminized. There may also be assumptions that all men are potential abusers of children. 'Should men work with children?' has been described as the 'most uncomfortable question of all' (Neustatter, 1993). The notion that it is unnatural for men to want to work with young children is underpinned by specific perceptions of masculinity. A response to such suspicions might be tighter screening procedures. Skelton disagrees and argues that this is in itself inadequate. She argues that 'the focus would be better placed on the interrelationship of masculinity, sexuality and violence and its implications for child abuse' (Skelton, 1994: 87).

Men working with young children occupy an ambivalent position made more difficult by narrow perceptions of what masculinity means. 'The man who is too "masculine" would be suspected of being an incompetent and insensitive teacher, while the man who is nurturing and empathetic would be stereotyped as feminine and "unnatural" (Allan, 1993: 126). Rather than working with one dominant version of masculinity, we should consider masculinities as 'constantly constructed within the history of an evolving social structure, a structure of sexual power relations' (Carrigan, Connell and Lee, 1987).

Therefore, what is said to be natural can take the debate in different directions. I want to argue that all of these perspectives, based explicitly or implicitly – yet often unproblematically – on what is natural, are unhelpful in moving the discussions forward. They hide rather than reveal the issues and they leave assumptions unexplored. they neither necessarily locate the debate within the discourse of equality and equity, nor base it on an understanding that recognizes gender as negotiated rather than fixed. What is necessary is an exploration of the underlying concepts of the natural in each case. One such exploration must consider the ways masculinity and femininity are understood.

Masculine and feminine: a natural dichotomy?

If masculine and feminine are taken to be homogeneous categories in opposition to one another, then much will be masked and the issue of power relations will not be foregrounded. Seifert is concerned with the differences between male and female biographies and 'how these differences facilitate female socialization into early education, but inhibit socialization for men' (Seifert, 1988: 70). His is an argument based on apparently unitary versions of male and of female within a theoretical framework of socialization as the means through which gender is learnt. This seems too rigid and simple an explanation. Carrigan Connell and Lee refer to an 'ideology of the "natural" differences between the sexes'

(1987: 46) and show how such an ideology reaffirms particular heterosexual versions of masculinity and denies homosexual versions. Segal
describes different versions of masculinity and identifies 'competing
masculinities' (1990: x), where sexuality and ethnicity are significant;
Segal argues that certain masculinities are dominant and have social
meanings that give them superiority over others and over women.
Differences between men, as well as the similarities between women and
men, should be acknowledged.

Perceptions of masculinity and the concept of care are related. Comments made by male students teachers who work with young children
suggest that 'interpretations of masculinity and identity will have a bearing on the ways they are able to demonstrate care, and the expectations
they have of themselves' (Smedley and Pepperell, forthcoming). Care has
the potential to be experienced differently by different people. Bernard
Misrahi, who worked as a nursery nurse, describes his perspective, 'I am
very close and physical with the children. It's my way of making them
feel secure and settled. ... Children will loose a great deal if we cannot
be natural with them' (Misrahi, ref. in Neustatter, 1993). For Misrahi,
demonstrating care through physical contact is 'natural' for him as a man.
However, there are tensions for men between predominant definitions of
masculinity and of care. It is important that there is dialogue about the
various definitions of masculinity in practice and that these are seen as
open to change, negotiation and transformation.

We need to ask whether there are particular 'masculine' ways that men
are expected to behave with children. Consider the following: 'It was
great for the children to have an alternative role model. ... He had loads
of energy and there was lots of rough and tumble playing – like climbing
trees' (Angie, ref. in Cook, 1997). This way of playing with children may
be perceived as typically masculine, but again this should be seen as
informed by one of many possible versions of masculinity.

In trying to understand how children learn to be boys or girls, we need
to be careful not to reinforce the stereotypes that we are trying to dispel.
It is not a simple question of providing role models; children learn gender
through complex interactions and negotiations in different contexts.

MacNaughton (1996) provides a post-structuralist argument to explain the ways children learn gender which may be helpful here. If one of our fundamental aims in working with young children is to work for equality and equity, then, MacNaughton argues, we must 'challenge children's stereotyped gender learning ... [by reconstructing] the gendered power effects of the discourses of masculinity and femininity through which children understand themselves and others' (MacNaughton, 1996: 22). Engaging children in dialogue, acknowledging their current play patterns, as well as offering other possibilities, are all important as ways forward.

The rhetoric of what is natural must be explored, or the inequalities and rigid differences between male and female might be reinforced, rather than challenged. There is an argument for exploring what is meant by 'natural' across a range of different cultural perspectives, analysing the assumptions that exist. Walkerdine suggests that 'we must view as *production*, rather than as an uncovering, those characteristics which define the normal and natural individual' (Walkerdine, 1983: 85). Changing the discourse will not change the wider context of inequality that still exists, but it may be a step in the right direction. Davies urges those working with young children to 'stop doing the work that maintains the difference' (1989: 136). She hopes that masculine and feminine will eventually be seen as 'archaic terms' (Davies, 1989: 141). Be that as it may, masculinity and femininity are complex and varied concepts, not fixed roles. The existing masculine/feminine paradigm must be changed (Miedzian, 1992). There is a need for a clearer understanding of masculinities and, within that, an understanding of the particular variety of masculinity that is hegemonic masculinity (Carrigan, Connell and Lee, 1987: 47). The discourse of masculinity must be a discourse of masculinities to acknowledge power relations and to acknowledge the diversity of ways men make sense of what it might mean to be a man working with young children.

Men and women who work with young children have a great responsibility. At a time when moves in the primary school sector suggest a prioritizing of skills and techniques in teaching, it is particularly important to give time and energy to promoting issues of social justice and the more affective side of education and care.

One outcome which I think is clear from these considerations is that gender plays a central role in our experiences and understanding and must remain a concern in discussing men and women working with young children. Goodman and Kelly (1988) and Skelton (1991) emphasize the importance of the context of equality and inequality. For Goodman and Kelly, 'The need is not for men who simply pass on the traditional male-centred culture unproblematically. To make a significant difference, we need more men who will mediate culture from an anti-sexist perspective' (Goodman and Kelly, 1988: 1). Skelton warns that without 'changes in attitudes, male power within education will become more deeply embedded' (Skelton, 1991: 288). Gender must be discussed within wider contexts of working for equality and equity (Smedley, 1996), taking into account the importance of the intersecting issues of social class and culture and recognizing of the historical and economic factors which are also part of the ways gender has influenced the lives and work of men and of women.

Note

1 I am writing from my perspective as a female tutor in primary initial teacher education with an interest in gender issues and, in particular, in male student primary teachers' experiences of moving into the primary school culture. Primary school teaching, like childcare services, is staffed mostly by women and many issues are relevant to both contexts.

References

Allan, J. (1993), 'Male elementary teachers. Experiences and perspectives'. In: C.L. Williams (ed.), *Doing 'Women's Work'. Men in Non-traditional Occupations.* Newbury Park: Sage.

Aspinwall, K. and Drummond, M.J. (1989), 'Socialized into primary teaching'. In: H. de Lyon and F. Widdowson Migniuolo (eds), *Women Teachers Issues and Experiences.* Milton Keynes: Open University Press.

Carrigan, T., Connell, B. and Lee, J. (1987), 'The "sex-role" framework and the sociology of masculinity'. In: G. Weiner M. and Arnot (eds), *Gender Under Scrutiny*. London: Hutchinson, in association with the Open University, Milton Keynes.

Cook, E. (1997), 'Would you let a gay man look after your child?', *Independent on Sunday*, Real Life, 30 March, 1–2.

Davies, B. (1989), *Frogs and Snails and Feminist Tales. Preschool Children and Gender*. North Sydney: Allen and Unwin.

Goodman, J. and Kelly, T. (1988), 'Out of the mainstream: issues confronting the male pro-feminist elementary school teacher', *Interchange, 19*, 2, 1–14.

Hockenjos, E. (1996), 'A good man is hard to find', *The Guardian, Society*, 20 March, 2.

MacNaughton, G. (1996), 'Is Barbie to blame? Reconsidering how children learn gender', *Australian Journal of Early Childhood, 21*(4), 18–24.

Miedzian, M. (1992), *Boys Will Be Boys. Breaking the Link between Masculinity and Violence*. London: Virago.

Miller, J. (1996), *School for Women*. London: Virago.

Neustatter, A. (1993), 'Should men work with young children?', *Independent on Sunday*, 25 April.

Oram, A. (1987), 'Inequalities in the teaching profession. The effect on teachers and pupils, 1910–39'. In: F. Hunt (ed.), *The Schooling of Girls and Women, 1850–1950*. Oxford: Basil Blackwell.

Segal, L. (1990), *Slow Motion. Changing Masculinities, Changing Men*. London: Virago.

Seifert, K. (1988), 'The culture of early education and the preparation of male teachers', *Early Child Development and Care, 28*, 69–80.

Skelton, C. (1991), 'A study of the career perspectives of male teachers of young children', *Gender and Education, 3*(3), 279–289.

— (1994), 'Sex, male teachers and young children', *Gender and Education, 6*(1), 87–93.

Smedley, S. (1996), 'Working for equality and equity'. In: S. Robson and S. Smedley (eds), *Education in Early Childhood. First Things First*. London: David Fulton Publishers.

— and Pepperell, S. (forthcoming), '"No Man's Land": caring and male student primary teachers', *Teachers and Teaching*.

Steedman, C. (1985), '"The mother made conscious": the historical development of a primary school pedagogy', *History Workshop Journal, 20*, Autumn, 149–163.

Vicinus, M. (1985), *Independent Women. Work and Community for Single Women, 1850–1920*. London: Virago.

Walkerdine, V. (1983), 'It's only natural: rethinking child-c
  A.M. Wolpe and J. Donald (eds), *Is There Anyone Here from*
  Pluto Press.
— (1985), 'On the regulation of speaking and silence: subjectivi
  in contemporary schooling'. In: C. Steedman, C. Urwin and V.   ᵥ (eds),
  Language, Gender and Childhood. London: Routledge & Kegan. raul.
Wallace, W. (1995), 'A man about the place', *Times Educational Supplement, TES 2,*
  13 October, 2–3.
Williams, R. (1983), *Keywords.* London: Fontana Press.

7 Men in Non-traditional Working Practices: What happens when men move into female-dominated occupations?

Sandy Pepperell
Roehampton Institute, London

As an introduction to this discussion about the effects of men moving into female-dominated occupations, I should like to describe briefly the work I am involved in and how it relates to this field. At Roehampton Institute, London, I have been working with Sue Smedley (we are both Senior Lecturers in Education) analysing the perceptions of male student primary teachers. We have focused on two main aspects: the way in which men relate to care in teaching and what might be the particular characteristics for which men are recruited. We have carried out in-depth interviews with students and analysed their perceptions with reference to literature and to public statements and documents on the recruitment of male teachers (Pepperell and Smedley, in preparation; and Smedley and Pepperell, forthcoming). My interest, in particular, relates to examining what is said to support increasing the number of male teachers and what issues male entrants experience on entry to a mainly female profession. Although the purpose of this chapter is to summarize the discussion of the seminar, I also wish to develop some points by referring to the case of primary teaching.

In discussing the question 'What happens when men move into female-dominated occupations?', it is first necessary to examine what is meant by 'female-dominated' occupations. Invariably this reflects a numerical imbalance rather than a tendency for women to occupy positions of authority in the occupation as a whole. For example, Sarah Robinson, in Chapter 5, gives the figure of 9 per cent male workers in nursing, while in researching numbers of men in primary teaching I have found the figure to be around 18 per cent. In addition to this, in both professions, men are concentrated in particular fields: in nursing, Sarah Robinson points out that men are disproportionately represented in the mental health field and, in teaching, DfEE statistics (1993) show more men working with older children and in management positions.

The presentations and subsequent discussion centred on:

- the difference in what happens when the number of men increases to make the numbers of men and women more equal:
- the need for an explicit discussion of gender issues;
- the status of work in the care professions and how status relates to gender;
- the value of international comparison.

Dealing with the first point, one key difference which arises is the contrast between a genuinely mixed-gender workforce and one in which there was a small number of 'token' males. The starting point in Erna Sundqvist's study in Sweden (Gothenburg) is a policy in the municipality to establish a mixed workforce in childcare. For nursing, Sarah Robinson suggests that the reasons for recruiting more men appear to be at least to some extent pragmatic, in that there are too few women entering nursing. In teaching, reasons for recruiting more men are usually related to role models for boys. Whatever the justification for changing the balance of gender of workers in the caring professions, however, it would appear that real change will only occur when a workforce is genuinely mixed. Erna Sundqvist's findings suggest that changes in general involve more the adaptation of women towards the men than *vice versa*. For example, topics of conversation were extended to include discussion of sport and politics as women joined in the 'male' conversations, but the men tended not to join in with the 'female' topics of conversation. Women workers felt they adopted a more direct way of speaking, from men. Although general feeling was positive, there were some negative effects: women felt men were more reluctant when it came to cleaning and it was felt that the men just wanted to 'do' rather than to spend time planning. The women tended not to mention what they did better. Both preferred the mix of genders and reported that there were fewer conflicts which were resolved more quickly.

When a small number of men is involved the 'token' male retains rarity value and can be seen in various stereotypical ways – in nursing, Sarah Robinson suggests that perceptions centre around sexuality (in particular the view that men who want to be nurses must be homosexuals), whether men *could* care and that men were only interested in promotion. All of these views were experienced, too, by the male student teachers in the Roehampton group I have interviewed. In Chapter 4, Johanna Lammi-Taskula suggests that children's activities with male care workers might become more physical and male workers might encourage more risk-taking. The stereotyping can be seen as positive for individual men in that men are believed to have special qualities, but at the same time it can be limiting, making it difficult to step outside accepted roles. In particular, this is a challenge in perceptions of risk of child abuse. In the genuinely mixed workforce, differences and similarities between individuals can be recognized and there may be an increased possibility for men and women to adopt a range of roles, for example some men *and* women might prefer to encourage more physical activity in both boys and girls, whereas others may feel more comfortable in supporting more contemplative activity. Others, again, may have strengths in a range of learning contexts.

On the explicit addressing of gender issues, Erna Sundqvist suggests that, although workers in her study were reluctant at first to do so, there was a need to address questions of preferred ways of working, relating to colleagues and whether there is anything special about what men and women do. Following policies to recruit more men, she proposes, it will not be sufficient to place men in these roles and expect change to occur. All workers need to address differences and similarities between them and to consider how a change in the gender composition of the workforce will change things.

Johanna Lammi-Taskula raises questions about the possibility of men entering 'female' occupations in significant numbers, unless the social context changed. She suggests that the maintenance of difference and hierarchy is more important to men and that this is reflected in things 'female' having less cultural prestige. She speculates that, because of associations with gender we might never see many more men in these professions. This casts doubt on the likelihood of any significant moves towards more gender-mixed workforces and extension of the changes noted in Erna Sundqvist's study.

According to Johanna Lammi-Taskula we need to look at changing definitions of masculinity and she describes a constant process of repro-duction and change so that new masculinities and femininities are being formed. Individuals play an active role in this, so that the men who work in 'female' professions will be making new versions of what work with children will be as well as new versions of what maleness can include. This makes notions of male workers as role models for boys problematic and in need of examination as to what the men in particular are expected to do. All of this reinforces Erna Sundqvist's points about discussing what differences there are in changing the current balance of gender in a workforce, but it also extends the analysis beyond the simple male/female dualism by examining what individuals bring to work with young children. Changing views about masculinity and femininity in the wider social context, she seems to suggest, can contribute to change in what is seen as appropriate work for men and women.

In the current context, it is often suggested that the status of caring professions such as nursing and teaching could be raised by recruiting more men. The fact that female-dominated professions are still mainly led or managed by men has significance for male workers in that careers are modelled in a way not experienced by women. Yet Kaupinnen-Toropainen and Lammi (1993) make the point that women are more likely to move into 'male' work than men are to move into 'female' work. Men may achieve more than women in female-dominated occupations, but not as well as men elsewhere. Pay and status were issues in deterring men, but it is not simply an economic matter. It is also a case of threat to masculine identity in entering what is seen as 'female' work. In the dis-cussion at the seminar examples were given of how the image of the

'Aunt' (for childcare worker) in Norway was off-putting for men in the same way it is suggested the title 'nurse' is. It was felt in general that work in services for young children is undervalued, that titles need revising (e.g. 'teacher' not 'Aunt') and that society and government need to value the work as the workers themselves do.

The status in work with young children is complex. As Johanna Lammi-Taskula suggests, it is related to the fact that it is seen as 'female' work, which has low value in society. Yet the suggestion that status could be raised by the recruitment of more men needs analysis. How will the status of women workers be raised by the increase in numbers of men? As Skelton (1991: 279) suggests, increasing the numbers of men could simply establish increased 'male power'. At the same time, how will men be attracted to a low-status occupation in order to raise its status?

A strong feature of the seminar as a whole was that the presentations allowed various comparisons: between countries, between occupations and with women entering male-dominated occupations. These comparisons were felt in the discussions to be valuable for putting issues in certain contexts into sharper focus by encouraging a fresh look at accepted structures and functions in work with young children. However, it was also felt that in making comparisons internationally, care should be taken with the potentially superficial nature of 'cultural borrowing'. There may be a particular combination of factors affecting the nature of work and experience of workers which are culturally specific, for example the way in which gender identities are formed might be different. This also applies, as Peter Moss (TCRU) pointed out in the discussion, to comparing different services even within one national context – childcare centres (the same could be said of schools) tend to be small units, whereas hospitals are larger and more bureaucratic organizations. This can be seen in the way that Erna Sundqvist has studied a childcare centre with relatively 'flat' management structure, one leader and everyone else on an equal grade, whereas Sarah Robinson describes the developed line management system usually found in hospitals. With these conditions made explicit, the comparisons were found to be enlightening and opened up new avenues of exploration.

In my own work with male student primary teachers, I found similar contradictions to those described by Sarah Robinson in people's perceptions of men who wish to take up nursing as a career. Attitudes encountered by men wishing to enter these occupations perhaps reveal the narrow assumptions held about the nature of work in the caring professions and about what constitutes masculinity. In relation to nursing, Sarah Robinson suggests that there is questioning, on the one hand, of male ability to care and about their masculinity and sexual orientation. On the other hand, it is suggested that men are only interested in promotion. Again, there are similarities between nursing and teaching about what men are expected to do once in the job, namely discipline in school and restraint in some aspects of mental health.

Just as international comparison can throw new light on particular contexts, comparisons with women entering male-dominated occupations can highlight some of the gender issues which need examination and explicit discussion if more positive policies are to be developed to recruit more men into 'female' occupations. For example, an increase in women in a 'male' occupation would not be seen to add to the existing dominance of women in management which is the fear in 'female' occupations. If it is seen as more 'natural' for men to want to be leaders in the caring professions, aims to increase their present indirect work with 'clients' (patients and children) will not succeed. Another example is given by Sarah Robinson in discussing privacy in the care of patients in hospital. This becomes an issue when it is suggested that male nurses should care for women, but it is less so when women care for men. Analysis must go beyond arguments for a simple fairness in numbers of men and women and include a recognition of the particular issues arising from men entering 'female' occupations.

In conclusion, discussion of the issues surrounding the question 'What happens when men move into female-dominated occupations?' needs contextualizing in the broader social context and can be informed by comparison between the different services and between countries.

In examining what happens when men enter 'female' professions (in numbers) two main changes occur:

- masculinity is changing, or there is a widening of the male/female dualism to include a range of gender identities to allow men the possibility of care work;
- the nature of the work changes.

In addition, it is often suggested that the work will be given added status with the increase of male workers. At the moment, services for young children are mainly staffed by women and there are only a small number of contexts in which there is a genuinely mixed workforce. It appears to be the case that explicit addressing of gender issues begins to highlight how men and women see their work differently. Will it be the men who adapt to 'female' work or will the work be changed to suit the male recruits? Who will ultimately benefit from these changes?

References

DfEE (1993), 'Full-time teachers in maintained nursery, primary and secondary schools – provisional data', 31 March.

Kaupinnen-Toropainen, K. and Lammi, J. (1993), 'Men in female-dominated occupations: a cross-cultural comparison'. In: C.L. Williams (ed.), *Doing 'Women's Work': Men in Non-traditional Occupations*. London: Sage Publications.

Pepperell, S. and Smedley, S. (in preparation), 'Calls for more men in primary teaching: problematizing the issues'.

Skelton, C. (1991), 'A study of the career perspectives of male teachers of young children', *Gender and Education*, 3(3), 279–289.

Smedley, S. and Pepperell, S. (forthcoming), '"No Man's Land?" Caring and male student primary teachers', *Teachers and Teaching*.

PART 3

Gender differences: What difference does it make having men working in services for young children – to children, parents and the staff group?

8 Gender Differences: The Child's Perspective

Charlie Lewis and Jo Warin
Lancaster University, UK

Introduction

In this chapter we will consider the child's perspective on the issue of men as workers in services (i.e. preschool education centres and day care) for young children. Given an imbalance in research, we will draw largely from the vast literature on the father–child relationship (for a review of paternal influence, see Lamb, 1997). Since the late 1960s thousands of papers have been written about men's involvement with preschoolers. For example, the PsycLIT database reveals that about 450 articles are published each year on fathers in journals with some connection with psychology. While these references are not exclusively from one discipline and are from many cultural and linguistic groups, we acknowledge that the dominant perspective is psychological and drawn from papers written in the English language. Nevertheless, we hold that it would be foolish to discard such a large database from our analysis of the effects of men on preschoolers' development.

We will draw on this literature to speculate on whether it makes any difference for the child to interact with men in preschool settings, both within and outside the family. We both have an affinity for beliefs about sexual equality at home and at work, so on the grounds of equal rights to both men and women, we would encourage the employment of men in preschool services. Nevertheless, we want to take the position of devil's advocate that, from the child's perspective, an increase in male involvement in services for children may not have any influence on their development.

Our argument is as follows.

- Within the home, as well as more visibly in preschool care and education settings, men are often noticeable by their absence. However, there is sufficient variability in men's domestic involvement to allow an examination the effects of paternal 'input' on the child's developmental 'outcome'.
- Studies of parent-child interaction suggest that we cannot isolate specific influences which men have on their children. Instead the data show that both men and women sex-type their children's behaviour and that there are some grounds for assuming that the context in which interaction takes place is more important than the sex of the adult.
- We have grossly underestimated the child's role in her or his own construction of gender and gender roles, and this will be illustrated with some data.
- As a result of the above, it can be seen that parents have a slight influence on their children's understanding of sex roles, but in many areas of development they have none.
- Some studies show that paternal involvement correlates with apparent 'enhancements' in children's development. However, the reasons for such links are open to question. When the crunch comes, paternal input does not appear to have a clear effect on children's development. The implications for the issue of men and child service provision are obvious.

Male absence from children's lives: a norm rather than an exception?

Men are largely absent from services for preschoolers and the last ten years have even witnessed a decrease in countries such as Sweden (Jalmert, personal communication, May 1997). They are also absent in many homes. In the United States, for example, national surveys show that, before they attend school, 40 per cent of preschoolers have lived at least part of their lives without their fathers (Mott, 1990). Even within two-parent families, many men appear to not to be involved in childcare. Although 'involvement' is hard to define, the figures speak for themselves. For example, an Australian study calculated that fewer than 2 per cent of fathers share childcare tasks equally with the mothers and the proportion of 'highly involved' men was under 10 per cent (Russell and Radojevic, 1992). Meanwhile 60 per cent of 'traditional' fathers had *never* looked after their children alone (Russell, 1983). The British National Child Development Study found that 43 per cent of fathers were reported to be out at work 'sometimes' or 'usually' until after the child's bed time (Osborn and Morris, 1982).

Figures such as these have been an impetus behind many moves to include men in services – the idea being that preschoolers should be exposed to the care of men to compensate for a father's absence. It has been assumed by some that children need a same sex model to imitate while learning the styles of their gender. Just why such an idea has been assumed for so long is interesting and needs more analysis. However, the psychological data show the following typical historical pattern. In the literature on divorce and young children, for example, the claim that children need a same-sex model seemed to be supported by the increase in behaviour problems in boys in single-mother households (Hetherington, Cox and Cox, 1982) and girls in single-father homes (Santrock and Warshak, 1979). However, as in many areas of family relationships, when all the data are collected, such effects appear not to be reliable – there is no clear sex of residential parent by sex of child influence in families after divorce (Downey and Powell, 1993).

Just because some households lack a male parent, while in others paid employment is a barrier to regular contact, does not mean that in all homes men are psychologically absent. The National Child Development Study, for example, found that in the week before they were interviewed 49 per cent of the fathers were reported to have participated in putting their four-year-old to bed (Osborn and Morris, 1982). The data on fathers in two-parent households shows that paternal contact with children and their involvement in childcare and home management are highly varied. This variance provides ample opportunity for modelling the nature and amount of paternal contact as predictors of what might be regarded as child 'outcomes', that is measures of the child's adjustment. Such outcomes can be examined in longitudinal designs, where potential precursors in parental attitudes, or actions (e.g. residence elsewhere, beliefs about child rearing or behavioural styles) are examined as predictors of how the children later feel about themselves, their success at public 'assessments' such as exam results, or their success at keeping out of trouble. We cite outcome studies not only because they give a temporal dimension to the research, but also because some are sophisticated enough to examine the complexity of influences over time such as the child's own contribution to her or his development.

Paternal influences on the child: the example of gender

There is a long-standing folklore in texts on preschoolers that fathers are important contributors to their children's development, particularly in their sex roles (e.g. Power, 1981), but also as an impetus to the children's cognitive development and motor skills, peer interactions and motivation for achievement (see Lewis, 1997, for a discussion). Certainly, there is evidence to suggest that fathers display greater control in their interactions with preschoolers, especially to their sons demonstrating more activities and less warmth (Bright and Stockdale, 1984). What effects do men have on their children? To answer this question, we could look at any of the areas discussed above, but let us consider sex-role development as it is the most heavily researched and theorized area of analysis.

As mentioned above there is an implicit assumption that children learn much about themselves and gender-appropriate behaviour by modelling or identifying with a same sex adult. Such a view is explicit in social learning theory and some psychoanalytic perspectives. Practitioners often refer to 'role models' to mean 'adult to copy' or 'adult to identify with'. What evidence is there to support such an assumption in the literature? It seems that simple cause–effect models implicit within the notion of a role model, are not supported by the evidence. Paternal style seems to be barely related to the child's social skills. This is demonstrated clearly in Lytton and Romney's (1991) meta-analysis of 172 studies of parent–child interaction. Seventy-seven per cent of the 27,837 children involved in these studies were preschoolers and the authors drew on a wide range of types of study, using observations, self-reports and other measures from a variety of types of research. Their analysis shows that there are many styles of mother–child and father–child interaction, but no obvious father–child patterns of influence. Effects which were significant in a minority of studies were non-significant in others. The only consistent factor to emerge from Lytton and Romney's analysis was men's encouragement of sex-typed activities, but their influence was less than half of one standard deviation – few men were sex typed in their choice of activities. If there were effects of history on Lytton and Romney's results, it was that differences between mothers and fathers were fewer in the 1980s than the 1960s.

A more consistent pattern in the research with preschoolers suggests that both mothers and fathers treat boys and girls differently. For example, Lytton and Romney found that both mothers and fathers engaged in sex-typed activities. The congruence between men and women in their interactions is evident even when factors within the child are taken into account. In one recent study of parent–child talk, for example, Reese and Fivush (1993) found that parents talked more and used more elaborate language with daughters than with sons. This was the case even though the boys had been shown to be as competent in their language skills as the girls. Reese and Fivush claim that, given that 'talk' is supposed to be a feminine activity, mothers and fathers respond to such stereotypes. An implication may be that a provider of services for young children will respond to social pressures and treat children in stereotypical ways (Delamont, 1980), irrespective of their own gender.

The literature on parent–child interaction reveals more than a consistent preference to treat boys and girls differently. It shows that the setting in which interaction occurs seems to be more important than the sex of the adult in interaction. Ross and Taylor (1989) examined parent–son dyads in two laboratory playrooms. One room contained stereotypically 'masculine' objects such as trucks and balls. The other contained 'feminine' toys such as books and puzzles. There were a few sex of parent effects, but the 'playroom influences' on both groups of parents' activities were stronger. In the 'feminine' playroom mothers and fathers engaged in more instructive and constructive play and reading, whereas in the 'masculine' room parents and children played more physical and pretence games. The children appeared to display greater positive effects when their parents adopted a 'masculine' style of play. So, if there were any apparent differences in the interactions of mothers and fathers with their preschoolers, these might reflect contextual rather than inherent differences between them. The goals of preschool provision may be more important than the personnel involved.

Infants' construction of gender: biological evidence

As the study of Ross and Taylor (1989) shows, in dyadic play with mothers or fathers, children's gestures to each parent were more influenced by the toys available in the playroom than the sex of the parent. These data raise the well-worn issue of how much the child contributes to both the way in which interactions take place and her or his own construction of gender. The evidence suggests that this contribution is a major one and we cite here some data to suggest that an attention to the differences between males and females occurs very early in development, despite the fact that many children (we presume) in these studies had limited experience of interactions with their fathers. The evidence in this section is provided to remind us that we need to be more aware of the child's construction of gender than is suggested in discussions about equal rights for adults in preschool services.

What do we know about young children's understanding of gender? Research over the last 20 years has suggested that infants are highly precocious in their ability to distinguish others on the basis of their gender. Even within the first months of life, children come to distinguish between male and female 'stimuli' (Leinbach, 1991). Studies employing techniques of visual preference (looking more at one of a pair of presented stimuli) or habituation (how long it takes to get used to a novel stimulus) reveal that by their first birthdays children become adept at discriminating the sexes. For example, when shown a succession of photographs of adults of one sex, a five-month-old will look longer at a new picture of an adult of the opposite sex than one of a member of the same sex, even when there are large individual differences between the photographs of men or women (Leinbach, 1991). Likewise, a seven-month-old (Miller, 1983) and perhaps even a two-month-old (Jusczyk, Mullinnex and Pisoni, 1992) will attend longer to the voice of an adult of one sex if she or he has previously listened to a member of the opposite sex. Such studies suggest that from a very young age babies show a basic discrimination between men and women.

While a two-month-old will show an ability to discriminate between pictures and sounds on the basis of gender, a one-year-old will show a preference for same sex stimuli even when she or her has minimal evidence to work on. Kujawski and Bower (1993) made a film of toddlers walking to and fro across a room in the dark, where all that could be seen were their joints moving as these were illuminated by luminous strips. Adults easily discern that the film is of an infant walking, but not the sex of the baby. However, one-year-olds reliably looked longer at other infants of the same sex, at least in first looks at pairs of moving stimuli presented simultaneously.

Sex role division in the preschool years: an alternative account

Kujawski and Bower's data suggest strongly that one-year-olds appear to have a preference for same sex pairs. If this is the case (and their data are greatly in need of replication and extension), this throws a different light on our understanding of why children seem to be sex-typed in their behaviour and peer preferences. The two predominant theories have been social learning theory and object relations theory. The former posits that children imitate the behaviour of same-sex models, whereas the latter suggests that (as a result of the highly sex-segregated divisions of responsibility for parenting) mothers implicitly rear their daughters to be like them and their sons to be 'unlike them'.[1] Both would imply that there is a need for men to have more visibility in services for young children. However, an alternative account, based on the claim that there is an inborn imperative to differentiate between the genders and to identify one's own gender (see below) would imply that there is no need for a greater male presence in the preschool years.

A biological model can explain why the patterns of gender differentiation appear so strongly across different family types and cultures. For a start, same-sex social interaction is found to increase with age from approximately two-years-old (and often before) to 11 – beyond the looking preference displayed by Kujawski and Bower. In the primary school years, the few occurrences of mixed-sex interaction are most likely to be the result of adult intervention. Left to their own devices, children do not usually choose to make new friends of the opposite sex. Where they are found to play with opposite-sex children, these are most likely to be relatives or friendships maintained from preschool days and supported by parents. It has even been reported that where such cross-sex friendships exist children feel it necessary to conceal them from their peers (Gottman and Parker, 1988). The occurrence of sex segregation between the ages of four and ten has been found in India, Okinawa, the Philippines, Mexico, Kenya and the United States (Whiting and Edwards, 1988), and in China, Japan, Bali, Kenya, India and the Kalahari (Freedman, 1980). There is a further difference between boys and girls in the form of sex segregation. Boys appear to play in large groups, whereas girls prefer more intense relationships with one or two 'best friends' (Maccoby, 1986; and Newson and Newson, 1985). Across these cultures, boys' play is characterized as being rougher, involving more fighting and more 'dominance-related' activity, and occurring in more public places. Girls' interaction involves more cooperation, turn-taking and exchange of confidences.

Sex-linked preferences spill over into children's understanding of the adult world. By their fifth birthdays children appear to have highly stereotypical views of parental roles. For example, Goldman and Goldman (1983) interviewed 838 five- to 15-year-olds across four different cultures about sex roles. In Sweden, 80 per cent of five-year-olds could think of a distinct role for mothers in the home, whereas only 50 per cent could think of such a role for fathers. Five-year-olds were more stereotyped than their older counterparts about the division of childcare responsibilities. They were adamant that mothers and fathers performed different domestic roles and were more stereotyped overall.

Do adults influence their children at all?

If biology compels infants to distinguish the categories of male and female from minimal sensory input, might such a prerogative account for the strong sex-typed preferences cited above? In the past, these patterns in children have been attributed to the exclusive care of preschool children by women. The way to test such an assumption is to examine whether any effects of parental input are discernible in children's understanding of sex roles. There is some evidence to suggest that parental attitudes (more than type of household, as might be expected) influence children's views. In dual-earner households, for example, the attitude of the employed mother has greater influence than her partner's attitudes in predicting whether or not the child appears to hold a sex-stereotyped view of adult roles (Baruch and Barnett, 1986). Given that women continue to provide the most input even when they work, it seems likely that their influence on children is greater. However, in families where the father is particularly nurturant and involved in childcare their preschoolers appear to attribute adults with fewer sex-role stereotypes (Carlson, 1984). Like others, Carlson found that boys were significantly more gendered in their attributions than girls. However, the sex stereotyping bias of boys was not found if their fathers shared in their care.

This evidence provides some support for the claim that children in different family types develop different values if one of their parents is committed to a particular point of view. However, these few studies have to be set against the many studies which show high sex stereotyping in children, with only slight variation across cultures (Goldman and Goldman, 1983)

The bottom line: are men important?

We suggested above that a wealth of studies has failed to show any discernible influence of the father on the child's development. In this section we want to argue, first, that the few exceptions to this rule can be explained away and, second, that there is now sufficient evidence to suggest that father-free development does not necessarily inflict harmful effects on preschoolers' development, even if services also 'deprive' children of contact with men.

Some data do suggest an influence of fathers on children's development. For example, Osborn and Morris (1982) found that paternal involvement in childcare related significantly to children's performance on a spatial motor task (copying designs) and verbal IQ. Does this demonstrate a positive effect of paternal 'input'? The answer has to be a guarded 'no'. For a start, the amount of predicted variance accounted for was obviously very low. More importantly, we have little grasp on the *causes* of such relationships, particularly given the failure of research to show differences between parents in their interactional styles. In our own research, we demonstrated significant relationships between paternal involvement in the primary school years and both the child's success at national examinations at age 16 and a smaller likelihood of obtaining a criminal record by age 21 (Lewis, Newson and Newson, 1982). However, such patterns might only tell us about family cohesion; they might reveal nothing about the input of the father *per se*.

What about families in which the father has been highly involved? The most detailed study which we have found is Radin's long-term analysis of 32 children aged 14–16, whose fathers had shared in their care during the preschool years (Williams, Radin and Allegro, 1992). This study produced a few significant associations between parenting responsibilities in the preschool period and the teenager's later sex-role attitudes. For example, where parents had reversed roles for some time in the child's early life, the teenager had less sex-stereotyped attitudes towards employment. However, high paternal involvement (i.e. role reversal or shared parenting) did not appear to change the teenager's attitudes towards sex roles in general.

If highly involved fathers do not inculcate lasting change in their children, what about families with no male involvement? Two types of family have been studied: those with lesbian parents (Golombok and Tasker, 1996) and single-parent families. The data on fatherless pre-schoolers have been examined in a meta-analysis by Stevenson and Black (1988). These show that once other factors are controlled, the effects of paternal absence seem to be less apparent than popular accounts suggest. One of the most extensive analyses (Crockett, Eggebeen and Hawkins, 1993) examined a large data set – the US National Longitudinal Survey of Youth. This sample contained over 1,500 preschoolers and younger parents and members of ethnic minorities were over-represented. Crockett, Eggebeen and Hawkins have examined the minute details of 'father absence', by breaking down the data set into finer subgroups, such as families where the father has resided continuously through the child's life versus those where a father figure resided either for the child's early life or in recent years, or never co-resided. Their analyses revealed that father absence was correlated with developmental problems. However, these effects were no longer in evidence when factors to do with the mother's social circumstances are employed as covariates. When her age and the family's poverty were controlled, there appear to be no unique contributions to the child's development made by the father's presence or absence (Crockett, Eggebeen and Hawkins, 1993).

Conclusions

In this chapter we have attempted to make a case that there are no *a priori* reasons for assuming that 'men' as a social category have any particular skills to impart on their preschool children. We could have made exactly the same case about 'women' as a social category. In making decisions about who looks after children, we feel that it is important to recognize that children make their own sense of the gender/culture of which they are part. They do not simply absorb values from mothers, fathers or service providers without evaluating and interpreting interactions. We feel it strange that the notion of 'role models' persists even though the theory on which it is premised (social learning theory) has been in abeyance for some years. Without a clear underpinning, such terms have little value.

We are not claiming that men have no effect on children, or that men cause more harm than good. On the basis of the literature from one discipline, we suggest that however hard psychologists have tried they have failed to identify a particular paternal influence on children. Although it might be the case that methods from other disciplines reveal more subtle effects, we feel that the available evidence supports our case. In many respects, the implications are positive. The data presented here lead to two conclusions. In the first place, preschoolers are highly discerning and construct an understanding of gender from very limited experience. Even in role-reversed families, the children appear to be as sex typed as those from families where the man is the only breadwinner. Second, the data explain why most children in families which differ from the stereotypical norm, the so-called 'traditional family' with the father as main breadwinner and mother as the primary care-giver (which itself has always been a minority type – see Rapoport, Rapoport and Strelitz, 1975), the children develop perfectly happily and normally. The issue of men's involvement in services providing young children's care and education must be understood within the wider goals of such provision. Our argument does not undermine the claim that greater involvement of men in preschool services would be better for both women and men.

Note

1. The most clearly articulated account of the object relations position is that of Chodorow (1978). She argues that the different psychic profiles of boys and girls can be located in the mother as the primary care-giver and 'love-object' of the newborn child. She claims that women's mothering brings about a different psychology in men and women, which repeats itself from one generation to then next. Mothering, as exclusive or at least primary care-giving, generates the needs and desires of girls to 'mother'. The process of individuation and differentiation from the mother is experienced differently by boys and girls. In order for boys to develop a separate and autonomous identity, they have to establish themselves as

being different from their mothers. Given that fathers are absent to a greater or lesser degree from primary childcare, the boy has difficulty in defining himself as male. His sense of maleness is constructed negatively, namely by what it is not. As the father may only be present for brief periods, the knowledge of masculinity that the child gains is necessarily limited and, therefore, likely to be much more stereotyped than the girl's equivalent sense of femininity derived from her mother. Thus, the boy has to resort to active rejection of the female as the most available strategy for discovering and asserting his sexual identity as a male.

Chodorow's theory can be criticized for the following reason. She bases her claims on a few case studies from psychotherapy. If her thesis is correct, then we would expect at the very least to see a closer attachment between the mother and infant, as opposed to the father and infant. More importantly, we would expect a closer link between mothers and daughters, particularly in terms of the predictions from mother– infant relationships to the child's later psychological adjustment. However, the accumulated studies suggest a high concordance between parents – if the child demonstrates security with one parent she or he is likely to have a secure attachment with the other in the 'Strange Situation' (Fox, Kimmerly and Schafer, 1991). Indeed, in families where the parents demonstrate close affection to one another early in infancy, the infant–parent attachments are significantly likely to be closer around the child's first birthday (Cox et al., 1992). Second, the research on the longitudinal effects of maternal attachments do not show a bias towards more secure and more influential mother–daughter attachments – attachments appear to be a-gendered (Lewis and Warin, in press).

References

Baruch, G.K. and Barnett, R.C. (1986), 'Fathers' participation in family work and children's sex-role attitudes', *Child Development, 57,* 1210–1223.

Bright, M.C. and Stockdale, D.F. (1984), 'Mothers', fathers' and preschool children's interactive behaviours in a play setting', *Journal of Genetic Psychology, 144,* 219–232.

Carlson, B. (1984), 'The father's contribution to childcare: Effects on children's perceptions of parental roles', *American Journal of Orthopsychiatry, 54,* 123–136.

Chodorow, N. (1978), *The Reproduction of Mothering.* Berkeley: University of California Press.

Cox, M.J., Owen, M.T., Henderson, V.K. and Margland, N.A. (1992), 'Predictions of infant–father and infant–mother attachment', *Developmental Psychology, 28,* 474–483.

Crockett, L.J., Eggebeen, D.J. and Hawkins, A.J. (1993), 'Father's presence and young children's behavioural and cognitive adjustment', *Journal of Family Issues*, *14*, 355–377.

Delamont, S. (1980), *Sex Roles and the School*. London: Methuen.

Downey, D.B. and Powell, B. (1993), 'Do children in single-parent households fare better with same sex parents?', *Journal of Marriage and the Family*, *55*, 55–71.

Fox, N.A., Kimmerly, N.L. and Schafer, W.D. (1991), 'Attachment to mother/ attachment to father: A meta-analysis', *Child Development*, *62*, 210–255.

Freedman, D.G. (1980), 'Sexual dimorphism and the status hierarchy'. In: R. Omark, F.F. Strayer and D.G. Freedman (eds), *Dominance Relations: An Ethological View of Human Conflict and Social Interaction*. New York: Garland S.T.P.M. Press, 261–271.

Goldman, J.D.G. and Goldman, R.J. (1983), 'Children's perceptions of parents and their roles: a cross-national study in Australia, England, North America and Sweden', *Sex Roles*, *9*, 791 – 812.

Golombok, S. and Tasker, F. (1996), 'Do parents influence the sexual orientation of their children? Findings from a longitudinal study of lesbian families', *Developmental Psychology*, *32*, 3 – 11.

Gottman, J.M. and Parker, J.G. (eds) (1988*), Conversation of Friends. Speculations in Affective Development*. Cambridge: Cambridge University Press.

Hetherington, E.M., Cox, M.J., and Cox, R. (1982), 'Effects of divorce on parents and children'. In: M.E. Lamb (ed.), *Non-traditional Families*. Hillsdale, NJ: Erlbaum, 233–288.

Jusczyk, P.W., Mullinnex, J. and Pisoni, D.B. (1992), 'Some consequences of stimulus variability on speech processing by 2-month-old infants', *Cognition*, *43*, 253–291.

Kujawski, J.H. and Bower, T.G.R. (1993), 'Same-sex preferential looking during infancy as a function of abstract representational', *British Journal of Developmental Psychology*, *11*, 201–209.

Lamb, M.E. (ed.) (1997), *The Role of the Father in Child Development (Third Edition)*. Chichester: Wiley.

Leinbach, M.D. (1991), 'The beginning of gender: What's happening before age two?'. Paper presented at the Society for Research in Child Development, Seattle, April.

Lewis, C. (1997), 'Fathers and preschoolers'. In: M.E. Lamb (ed.), *The Role of the Father in Child Development (Third Edition)*. Chichester: Wiley, 121–142.

Lewis, C. and Warin, J. (in press), 'Mothers, fathers and early sex roles'. In: C.A. Niven and A. Walker (eds), *The Psychology of Reproduction, Volume 3*. Oxford: Butterworth Heinemann.

Lewis, C., Newson, E. and Newson, J. (1982), 'Participant fatherhood and its relationship with career aspirations and proto delinquency'. In: N. Beail and J. McGuire (eds), *Fatherhood: Psychological Perspectives*. London: Junction, 174–193.

Lytton, H. and Romney, D.M. (1991), 'Parents' differential socialization of boys and girls: A meta-analysis', *Psychological Bulletin, 109*, 267–296.

Maccoby, E.E. (1986), 'Social groupings in childhood: their relationship to prosocial and antisocial behaviour in boys and girls'. In: D. Olweus, J. Block and M. Radke-Yarrow (eds), *Development of Antisocial and Prosocial Behaviour: Research Theories and Issues*. New York: Academic Press, 263–284.

Miller, C.L. (1983), 'Developmental changes in male/female voice class of classification by infants', *Infant Behaviour and Development, 6*, 313–330.

Mott, F.L. (1990), 'When is a father really gone? Parental–child contact in father absent homes', *Demography, 27*, 499–517.

Newson, E. and Newson, J. (1985), 'Family and sex-roles in middle childhood'. In: D.J. Hargreaves and A.M. Colley (eds), *The Psychology of Sex Roles*. London: Harper and Row.

Osborn, A.F. and Morris, A.C. (1982), 'Fathers and childcare', *Early Child Development and Care, 8*, 279–307.

Power, T. (1981), 'Sex typing in infancy: the role of the father', *Infant Mental Health Journal, 2*, 226–240.

Rapoport, R., Rapoport, R.N. and Strelitz, Z. (1975), *Fathers, Mothers and Others*. London: Routledge and Kegan Paul.

Reese, E. and Fivush, R. (1993), 'Parental styles of talking about the past', *Developmental Psychology, 29*, 596–606.

Ross, H. and Taylor, H. (1989), 'Do boys prefer daddy or his physical style of play?', *Sex Roles, 20*, 23–33.

Russell, G. (1983), *The Changing Role of Fathers*. Milton Keynes: Open University Press.

Russell, G. and Radojevic, M. (1992), 'The changing role of fathers? Current understandings and future directions for research and practice', *Infant Mental Health Journal, 13*, 296–311.

Santrock, W.J. and Warshak, R.A. (1979), 'Father custody and social development in boys and girls', *Journal of Social Issues, 35*, 112–125.

Stevenson, M.R. and Black, K.N. (1988), 'Paternal absence and sex-role development: A meta-analysis', *Child Development, 59*, 793–814.

Whiting, B.B. and Edwards, C.P. (1988), *Children of Different Worlds: The Formation of Social Behavior*. Cambridge, Mass.: Harvard University Press.

Williams, E., Radin, N. and Allegro, T. (1992), 'Sex role attitudes of adolescents reared primarily by their fathers', *Merrill Palmer Quarterly, 38*, 457–476.

9 Men as Workers in Services for Young Children: Issues of a Mixed-gender Workforce

Trevor Chandler
Pen Green Centre

Introduction

The Pen Green Centre is a multi-disciplinary provision for children under the age of five and their families. The Centre aims to provide open and equal access to all families in the local community. It is open 48 weeks a year, offers an extended day, and is an integrated jointly funded service (i.e. has the involvement of all three principal agencies concerned with children's education, social welfare and health and development).The centre provides nursery education and day care and a variety of support services to families, including community education and support groups.

The Centre has been involved in working on gender issues for many years. This has involved both actively encouraging the appointment of male childcare workers and working with staff and parents to encourage the increased involvement of fathers in family life and in the Centre. This has included staff training on values and attitudes towards men in the caring role, practical ways in which we can involve fathers more and discussions with parents on the role of men in childcare.

Examples of training are:

- working with men using an external consultant to look at staff issues;
- training on gender issues in the nursery;
- male staff (three men) running a seminar for female staff (16 women);
- in service training through staff meetings on a regular basis;
- male and female parents involved in EU seminars and discussions;
- discussion groups with parents using questionnaires;

- organization of the national men as carers;
- a gender training day organized for the county.

The nursery practice issues which arise, include:

- an anti-sexist approach in nursery practice/nursery curricula;
- a men's group;
- a conciliation group;
- women's assertiveness groups;
- the involvement of fathers in a nursery record-keeping project;
- an increased use of groups by men, including mixed-gender groups;
- a display campaign on positive images of men.

In terms of employment, the Centre:

- employs unqualified men on government employment schemes;
- recruits male social work and nursery nurse students, and community service volunteers;
- had a successful bid to the European Social Fund for working with unemployed men who want to get into childcare;
- positively recruits men onto the staff;
- encourages fathers to undertake National Vocational Qualifications.

The Centre holds meetings with parents on what would make it easier for men to use the nursery and has made a video made on how to greet the parents of nursery children. It also conducts research on:

- fathers' employment patterns and how they affect fathers' involvement in the care of their children;
- parents' employment and marital status;
- mothers' employment and life histories.

The Centre's policies include:

- evening crèches and babysitting to enable fathers to attend groups and meetings;
- that some groups must be run as single gender groups;
- that groups of men should always have at least one male group leader;

- that all meetings with parents should offer morning, afternoon and evening times to enable working parents to attend;
- that there should be home visiting when fathers are at home;
- an equal opportunities statement.

(Taken from M. Whalley (1996), *Men as Carers*.
Report on Ravenna Seminar, March.)

Men as childcare workers: a study

For the purposes of the seminar, I interviewed 30 people at the Centre, including two male childcare workers (one is a full-time qualified family worker who has worked at the Centre for four years, the other is a Danish student on placement for six months), parents who have children in the nursery (some parents have a male family worker others a female family worker) and the staff group.

I asked the following questions (adapted according to the interviewees).

- What are the benefits of having male childcare workers for you?
- What are the barriers to, and worries or inhibitions about having male workers?

Response of the staff group

Of the 20 staff present, three were male workers, one of whom was Danish. One female member of staff is from Japan and another from Germany. The staff group consisted of family workers (including teachers and nursery nurses), social workers, project workers, community service volunteers and students. The staff were divided into small groups on an *ad hoc* basis to discuss set questions, followed by general discussion and feedback in the large group.

The points raised can be divided into three main categories plus some general points.

The first category was children, where:

- it was the general belief that children have a right to experience a caring and healthy relationship with men as well as women;

- the belief was that children should see and experience healthy and creative relationships between men and women on the staff team;
- all the men on the staff group found that children expected them to play rough and tumble games; they did not want to be put in this role all the time and had to negotiate with the children to participate in other calmer activities;
- it was, however, considered important by the male workers that they hung onto the 'wild side' of their play and not be submerged into the female-dominated culture;
- all the staff considered it important to value the gender differences in the way they related to children, in other words an all-female or all-male approach was not good for children, nor was androgyny realistic or desirable;
- the men's sense of humour with children was different.

In the second category of staff, the view was that:

- interpersonal relationships between staff and their personalities was more important than gender difference in terms of whether discussion was affected or inhibited;
- personality and style of leadership was more important than gender;
- the importance of a common and shared philosophy of practice was more important than gender;
- gender difference was an important factor, but it was often intangible and hard to articulate (there would always be a 'gap' between men and women as they experience the world and themselves differently and identify with their own gender.

In the category of parents, points raised included that:

- fathers come in more often and stay longer and they seem to be more comfortable;
- women survivors of sexual abuse who have children in nursery said that they want their children to experience a safe, caring and healthy relationship with men; they want their children to experience something that they have not had;

- children of single-parent mothers or from families which have experienced abusive/destructive relationships with fathers benefit from a positive role model of caring males.

Other issues that were identified as important were:

- the dynamics of minorities in groups where they can be either excluded or submerged into the larger group;
- having male workers in early years settings in itself challenges gender stereotyping; childcare (especially in early years) is not valued highly enough and may become more so if more men were involved;
- it is important for men and women to recognize the masculine *and* feminine within themselves as well as valuing their own gender.

The response of male workers

The two workers interviewed shared some common beliefs and experiences. Both came into childcare because they felt that it was important for children to experience a safe and caring relationship with a man. Imparting values about caring for yourself and others was important. Providing a positive model of men for both girls and boys was also seen as important. One worker had a very positive and influential relationship with a male care worker and, for him, there was a lot of satisfaction in the prospect of children remembering him years after he had stopped being their care worker. Both workers were part of the community within which they worked and felt that this played an important part in their acceptance by parents in caring for their children. One worker thought that boys did relate to him differently as a male worker and he felt that it was important for him to maintain a balance between his 'wild' side and his caring side.

For one worker maintaining his male identity was not an issue, but for the other worker it was. He was afraid that women would 'slide into [his] brain and make [him] more feminine'. He felt that it was important to hang onto and value his maleness.

The response of parents

Parents who were interviewed included a single-parent father who had a male family worker. He found it very helpful to have a male worker because he felt judged by women and felt that he had to prove himself as a parent. He saw his family worker as 'laid back' and non-judgmental. He didn't feel pressurized or feel the need to prove himself. He also felt that his son, who was in nursery, related well to his family worker and benefited from a positive male role model. However, he did add that if he had had a daughter to look after he would prefer to have a female family worker.

Mothers who had a male family worker also felt that their children were benefiting from a male care worker. One mother who has three daughters felt that her family was too female-dominated and having a male worker helped to provide a balance. Her husband also worked long hours and did not have a lot of time with the children. She stated, 'My family worker provides consistent and positive contact for my daughter.'

Another important factor for parents was whether their children felt happy with their family worker. They saw their male family worker as very approachable and did not feel that there was any subject that they could not discuss with him because he was a man and not a woman. One mother said that she had one daughter in nursery who was very feminine and 'girlie' who had a female family worker and that she had benefited from this, rather than having a male worker. Her other son and daughter had a male family worker and related very well to him.

Mothers who had a woman as a family worker also welcomed having men working in the nursery. They thought that it provided a positive role model for children. One mother felt that having men working in the nursery was good provided that police checks were made and that every effort was made to ensure that the man appointed was safe. Several parents said that they knew Pen Green Centre well and trusted its judgement in appointing staff who were safe and that it provided high-quality care and education for their children.

10 Masculine Care: The Nursery School as a Man's Workplace

Tommie Nilsen and Lars Manum
Hauketo Barnehage, Oslo, Norway

Introduction

'The nursery school as a man's workplace' project is a continuation of the 'Focus on the man in nursery school' project, in which both of us participated. This led to another project with the government. Our goal for the future is to achieve a balance of 50 per cent women and 50 per cent men working in services for young children throughout Norway.

The starting point of our work was a desire to show how good the nursery school is as a workplace. We want to highlight the work we have each been doing for 27 and 15 years respectively and in which we both plan to stay. We want to present our work in such a way as to encourage other men who are in a situation where they have to make career or employment decisions to say, 'Maybe this is something for me?'.

Our motivation comes from an interest in children's development, their upbringing and 'quality childhood' (see Ministry of Children and Family Affairs (1996), *Framework Plan for Day Care Institutions: A Brief Presentation*. Q-0917 E. Oslo: Barne-og familiedeparetementet).

The situation in Norway – yesterday and today

Childhood in Norway today is almost entirely institutionalized. To counter this serious situation, there needs to be a conscious effort to recruit more men to jobs in nursery schools. We believe men have much to offer in relation to a child's development – by which is meant care, upbringing, playing and learning.

We are concerned with how our own experience of childhood development affects us as adults: how we are, our behaviour, our social attitudes, our values and our view of nature. Most people who work in nursery schools had a different childhood from the modern version. This is maybe because they did not go to nursery school and grew up free of adult supervision and control.

When we look back on how we grew up, we remember the older children in our communities who were the 'teachers', and who showed us the possibilities which surrounded us – in the meadows, in the old harbour gardens and in the forest ('our forest', 50 metres from our front door).

They took us along with all our faults. Our desire to learn was insatiable and our ability to learn was brilliant because the process itself was crucial. Everything had to be conquered. The home was our security – the place where we soaked up nourishment and care before heading out into the world as the great conquerors and explorers.

We have always chosen to use 'nature' as one of the most important instruments in our daily work with children's playing and learning. We believe that children learn just as well outdoors as indoors. Nature is one of the few areas in which children can still play, explore and learn by themselves, in their own way.

In today's society there are many gaps in children's lives, for example in the family and between the generations. In our view, one of the most serious gaps is that between preschool children and seven- to 12-year-olds. Adults will never be such good educators as seven- to 12-year-olds are in passing on children's culture. Children's culture and everyday skills are constantly being handed on with power and identity from child to child. This is a constant state of change, some things are lost, while new things are gained. The time that children of different ages are spending together is reducing.

We are concerned about the potential consequences of this change. We believe that if we take opportunities away from children, we are taking away their chance of teaching themselves important everyday skills.

Many adults today ask themselves why children do not play where they used to. What has happened to the forest ? The pathways from the

old days are all overgrown. We believe the reason is that the seven- to 12-
year-olds of today have also attended nursery school, been in day care
with few other children or have been almost alone with their mothers. In
our view, too little attention has been paid in the nursery school to
teaching children everyday skills.

The challenge to the nursery school as an institution

How successful are adults working in nursery schools in translating their
good experiences from when they were children themselves into their
work? The nursery school today is full of children who do not know what
to do in the snow when it first falls.

When we think about what kind of children we want to bring up, we
consider what kind of adults we want them to be in contact with. What
kind of experiences do we want to pass on to children?

Everyone who did not go to nursery school learned from someone how
to build snowmen and play in the snow. We want adults to experience
things with children, to play in the snow and show children how things
are done. Adults who are closely connected to their once childlike ways,
and can demonstrate this to children, are in our opinion attractive play-
mates for children.

Adults who manage a balance between being closely connected to
their childlike ways and, at the same time are clearly being adult, are in
our view a good child-rearers and educators. Being able to move in and
out of one's own age group – an experience in itself – makes the adult in
question qualified to adopt the *teaching role* of other children .

We want adults who are interested in co-experience and in being
creative with children. They should have a unique interest, commitment
and curiosity in relation to the child they are busy with at any given time.
This can help give the child some of the same sense of freedom that we
ourselves experienced as children. It is a sense of freedom we want to
give the individual child within the framework of the nursery school and
its possibilities. For us, it is about freedom with *responsibility*, and that
requires the *involvement* of adults.

Stopping the violence, starting in the kindergarten

One of the most important things in bringing up children is to see care in the context of the increased violence and other antisocial, self-destructive attitudes in society. As men in a kindergarten, we want to stand up and say 'No' to this violence. Social responsibility, care, involvement with and respect for other people are values in our society. In our opinion, society has a major problem with transferring positive values from generation to generation.

The explanation for increased violence is complicated. The absence of men as role models, such as fathers or other distinct male role models is part of the explanation. Therefore, we think that it is important to promote the employment of young men in the care of young children. In a way, care is the opposite of violence. More men in childcare services will, probably, lead to more caring fathers. These fathers will then again be good models for the next generation of fathers. We have experienced that this leads to more care among the other fathers in their neighbourhood. Perhaps this could be an interesting field for research?

Involved adults

Berit Bae, who works as a researcher in the education of nursery nurses in Oslo, has described the *absence of adults* as being one of the main problems of the nursery school. What does she mean by this? She herself says that children need adults who are *sufficiently close to children's experience.*

In Norway we are today facing a generation of parents without a model. Parents today are not readily able to give their own children the upbringing they themselves received from their parents. Society is changing faster nowadays than it did 30 or 40 years ago. Everything has become more specialized, and adults have to keep themselves informed with what is going on in the different areas in society. When our parents were children, they were receiving much the same upbringing that their parents had received from their parents. The problem now is that they cannot pass this way of bringing up children to their own children. Children today are learning things that their parents don't know, for example knowledge of computers.

Children needs heroes, and if we ask adults today who were their heroes when they were young, they will often answer their teacher, their mother or father, or cartoon heroes. One of the reasons they admired these people was as a result of identifying with them. An important question adults ask children is, 'What will you do when you grow up?' The expected response is that the boys will be firemen and the girls will be nurses or nursery nurses. What kind of a man wants to be a nursery nurse? In our dictionaries there was no expression like 'preschool teacher'. We believe that the staff in the kindergartens can be the children's heroes – adults with whom children want to identify.

Children learn through mastering things. They charge through life with a raging appetite to be successful and to get things done. Are those who work in nursery schools concerned about getting the relationship right, and sharing in the fascination in such a way that they too are able to experience this feeling? These adults need the following attributes.

- To satisfy a child's need for warmth – this is to recognize when children are down and in need of comfort, support and encouragement. They recognize when children need a lap to sit on – when life and their best friends are against them.
- To recognize a child's need to master – this is a concern that children should succeed and achieve that for which they are striving. Children need adults who show respect and give praise for their efforts.
- To be an adult in a way with which the child can identify. We have dealt above with how this generation of parents has no role models. Children need role models; they need adults who act and behave in a certain way, so that the child says, 'That's how I'm going to be when I grow up!'
- To be willing to fight for, and recognize, the child's potential. There are many children in nursery schools and schools in Norway who need support. These are children often have anti-social or deviant behaviour

patterns. Although it is a difficult and tough job, these children do need adults to fight their corner so they can learn a socially acceptable way of behaving.

- To stand up as adults in relation to children's behaviour. We believe that many of children's behavioural problems stem from them being faced with making choices they cannot cope with. This also means that adults have to be able to say 'no', knowing full well that shortly afterwards (when the child has screamed, hit, sobbed or cried for long enough), they will be able to say 'yes'.

Conclusions

We have described what children need to learn and this should have consequences for how adults behave when they are with children.

This is how we try to work every day, with children, staff and parents. The result in Steinbråten Kindergarten is that there are eight men in a total staff of 18 and in Hauketo kindergarten there are five men in a total staff of 20.

11 Men as Workers in Childcare Services: A European Perspective[1]

Jytte Juul Jensen

Jydsk Paedagog-Seminarium, Risskov, Denmark

Introduction

You will find male workers in some of the wonderful day nurseries for under-threes in Barcelona. In Madrid, I met a male dressed up as an Indian in a centre for under-six-year-olds. In an outlying village in Portugal, you will find a very engaged male trained worker (the first man trained to work with young children in Portugal, where it was forbidden for men before the Carnation Coup in 1974), who, together with a female trained worker, runs a kindergarten, which is deeply involved in the local community. In Northern Italy there is a nursery school playground resembling a park, in which there are fantastic experiments with water, ingenious technical constructions, a little lake for birds – and, sure enough, here a male trained staff member has left his mark. In a kindergarten in Brazil I peeped into the children's sleeping room, and there sat a newly employed man, trying very carefully and gently to get a new little girl to sleep – and that can be difficult. An influential Brazilian researcher has started to write about this issue. A Japanese researcher turns up in Denmark and Sweden, because she has heard about our engagement in and practice with male staff in our childcare centres. In Greece, I ask the head of the university department training childcare workers in Athens, how many male students she has. She laughs and asks, 'What male students?' In Great Britain, there is a childcare centre in Sheffield with equal numbers of male and female staff employed, and also men from many different cultural backgrounds. Yet in Britain, every time the issue of men as workers in nurseries is raised, one ends up discussing, very seriously, if many of the male workers will seek work in childcare centres just to abuse the children. This is the opinion of influential people, some of whom would even forbid male staff to be employed. Yes, even in Britain, one imagines oneself on another planet!

On the European stage, men as carers are on the agenda. The debate on the role of fathers has been the main focus so far, and fathers have even had their own year under the auspices of the United Nations. Many men do, of course, become fathers, whereas very few men take part in the public caring for younger children.

The Nordic approach has been that it is important to increase the number of men working with young children. Children need both men and women workers. Men are accepted as workers on the same basis as women, although it is recognized that men and women may have different ways of working with children. The discussion has been about *how* to increase numbers.

In Britain, however, the debate has been much more equivocal, focusing on the risk of child abuse in childcare and other services and whether employing men increases that risk. The discussion, therefore, has been about *why* and *if* men should be employed in childcare services.

In the European Union (EU) countries south of Denmark the characteristics are more the absence of men and a lack of debate and general policy on the issue.

This chapter is based on my ten years' work in the European Commission Network on Childcare and other Measures to reconcile Employment and Family Responsibilities (referred to here as the EC Childcare Network), for which I was the Danish member. The EC Childcare Network consisted of one member from each EU country and a coordinator. The tasks were to advise the Commission about, and to make analyses of, how working life and family life can be better reconciled. The Network had its authority in the EU's Action Programmes on Equal Opportunities for Women and Men. The Network concluded its work in 1996 (EC Childcare Network, 1996a). For some years we gave priority to the role of men as fathers and in other caring roles. I prepared a publication *Men as Workers in Childcare Services – a Discussion Paper*[2] (1995). In this chapter possible answers are given as to why it is important to get more men employed in childcare services. It also raises a number of discussion points and gives examples of good practice.

The EU has fathers and men as carers on the agenda. In the White Paper on Social Policy, the Commission argues that 'greater solidarity between men and women is needed if men are to take on greater responsibility for the caring role', and commits itself to 'looking at ways of addressing the issues of stereotype roles of the sexes in society'. In the Council Recommendation on Childcare, adopted in March 1992, member states committed themselves to 'promote and encourage, with due respect for freedom of the individual, increased participation by men [in the care and upbringing of children]' (Article 6).

The EC Childcare Network has taken the clear position that more men should be employed. It has led to the Network's proposal that a target of 20 per cent male workers should be reached over the next ten years (EC Childcare Network, 1996b).

This chapter will examine some reasons *why* it is important to employ more men in childcare services and consider the case in terms of children, staff, parents, men themselves and the labour market, including equal opportunities reasons. In addition, it will consider what policies might encourage and support more male recruitment and retention in childcare services.

Why men in childcare services?

Childcare centres do not have too many women, but they have too few men!

For the sake of the children

The main reason for getting a gender balance among workers in childcare services is that it will improve the quality of the daily life for the children – both boys and girls – in childcare services. This could also help develop in the children a sense of equality.

The reason is not that boys – because of the lack of male care and of male role models – will later become violent criminals, although that has been argued in Denmark. What about childhood in the 1950s and 1960s, when children grew up at home with mummy, and daddy worked many hours outside the home? Those children should also have become criminal and violent. No, the reason is that it will give them a better childhood *here and now.*

Getting more men employed in childcare services should also take place in order to assure the *rights* and *needs* of children. In the UN Declaration on children's rights, children are assured of their rights to have contact with two parents, so why should children not have this right in the social care sector as well?

Gender pedagogy

The fact that boys and girls are different in some ways and choose different games and activities gives different challenges to those employed – both female and male – in childcare centres. The daily pedagogic work must take these differences into account if the needs of both boys and girls are to be met.

For a long time, gender-neutral practices were seen to be the ideal, where boys and girls were given the same opportunities. With the recent debate about the 'unruly boys' in the four- to six-year-old group, new signals were given, and many saw the employment of men in childcare as a solution to the problem. Here, the gender of both the children and the staff came into focus. Later, the focus was widened to the 'gentle girls': girls should also be given special attention.

How do the pedagogues and other workers in childcare services feel about this difference between boys and girls? Is there a difference in the way female and male employees react to it? Research tells us very little. The discussion of the unruly boys has been the focus. However, as the child researcher Jan Kampmann wrote in the newspaper *Dagbladet Information* in 1995:

> Even though boys are more difficult and noisy, they are the ones that the adult pedagogues – here the female – think are lovely. At first, the girls may benefit from the adult females' feelings of recognition, but, in

this recognition, there is not always respect for the value of their ability to respond to the complete range of feelings? On the contrary, the pedagogues are actually irritated more by the girls.

The only research that I have found about how boys and girls are affected when an equal number of men are employed shows that girls are actually more affected by the presence of male staff (Carlquist, 1990).

In Denmark today, we talk about gender pedagogy in which it is emphasized that specific gender behaviour must be reflected in pedagogic work. These considerations must apply whether there are only females, a few males or many males employed – in other words, irrespective of the gender mix of the staff. In general, the philosophy is that respect is shown for all children, both boys and girls, and for their different needs. The adults should create exciting and inspirational surroundings, so that there is room for the activities of both boys and girls.

Furthermore, the adults must, in their choice of activities, be aware of the gender aspect. Some childcare services consciously create gender-divided activities where boys and girls are separated, based on the principle that the difference must be made in order to create equality. One childcare centre in Denmark is now talking about 'caring boys' and 'loud girls'. Here the aim is that girls should learn to say 'No' and that boys should learn the 'role of caring'. Gade and Larsen (1997) describe a project in a childcare centre, which was 'established as a counter reaction against the one-sided focus which until now has been on boys, and to focus the attention on girls' opportunities for development and self-realization in childcare centres'. It is important that both men and women in childcare centres experiment with different strategies. No one solution is always the right one.

These policies and recommendations for action can hardly be fulfilled in a childcare setting where there are only female staff. They can more easily be fulfilled in a mixed-gender work group that will contain a greater diversity of masculine and feminine traits than a single-gender group. It is also clear that female workers can never replace men as 'identification figures', nor can many of them show interest in rough/wild games in the same way that many male workers can – yet these are a vital part of the activities in any centre. The employment of men is not only a question of a traditional division of work between men and women. Both men and women do care, but they have different caring cultures and do it in a different way.

For the sake of staff cooperation

In 1988 Gothenburg in Sweden opened an equal rights childcare centre where equal numbers of men and women were employed. A researcher examined the consequences for staff cooperation (Granath-Sundqvist, no date).

The presence of men influenced staff teamwork, in that conversation was improved to be both different and broader, with subjects such as politics. However, the women still talked about women's subjects without the men joining in. At the same time, the way of communicating changed: men are more direct and this was appreciated by the women. Problems were solved more quickly. The typical way in which women communicate – turning things round and round, backwards and forwards, and being fearful of saying things directly and thereby causing a conflict – disappeared. Both men and women found the childcare centre, with its equal numbers of male and female staff, unusually free of conflicts. The women adopted the male way of talking to one another without feeling that they were subordinating themselves. They really felt that it was better. As it said in the report: 'How constructive is it to continue to call it subordination? Is it not just something that women come to think of as better? And is this not what equal rights supporters have been looking for in vain from male bosses for many years, namely an appreciation of the specific femininity?' In this centre you can find strong women with a powerful job identity, and this change must be recognized as a positive innovation. Women know what they want to do and how they will do it and maintain it too, even though men may have other ideas.

Another thing that is striking is the way that men are accepted in childcare services. It is completely different from the way women are accepted at workplaces dominated by men. Everybody is positive towards the male pedagogues, particularly the female pedagogues. Some of the women have even applied for a job in this particular childcare centre in order to be able to work together with men. None of them will go back to working in a single-sex workplace. Research into women entering male workplaces shows the opposite: many men leave and the work in question attains a lower status.

One of the central elements in good teamwork is that there should be more than one man employed in a childcare centre. A single swallow does not make a summer! Otherwise a man can easily feel himself left out in the cold and the male culture will find it difficult to break through. A solitary man can easily get the status of being something special (a 'token' man). He becomes isolated and is excluded from the team. This is why it is important to employ more than one man.

As more men are employed, they will provide a counterculture to the traditional cultures of childcare centres. Centres can no longer ignore the male way of doing things. The male culture can be a magic mirror for the female pedagogue. As men have other ways than women, it will be necessary to discuss routines, rituals, regulations and so on. In this way, employment of men can be seen as providing a potential for development of centres and can be a dynamic factor in the centres' culture.

For the sake of the parents

Most parents (including single parents) are positive about having male workers in childcare centres. Many fathers are pleased with the male presence. It can be easier for men to establish good contact with fathers. 'Man's talk' is used to achieve this contact.

For the sake of the men

Like boys and girls, male and female pedagogues are individuals, each with his or her own characteristics, but it is easy to over-generalize with regard to men (and women). Some of the generalizations made about men can easily become disadvantages for male workers. They can be expected to adopt a traditional masculine gender role by the female workers, the children and the parents. For example, they can be regarded as unqualified to work with (young) children and be expected to love playing football and taking part in other physical activities and workshop activities. Several female pedagogues have told me that they have had a man appointed in their centre, but that he was not a 'real' man. Shall 'real' women also only be employed?

In a UK study of family centres (Ruxton, 1992), almost all the male workers were pushed into being 'supervisors'. Men are expected to behave in the traditional, disciplinary male role: 'They didn't want me because they wanted a caring man, they wanted me primarily as a strong disciplinarian father-figure' (Hill, 1990). The author of this UK study also points out that a man's gender role and masculinity will also be affected by his ethnic and class background, and, of course, this is also the case for women and children in childcare centres.

For the sake of the labour market

It is difficult to find statistics about the gender of the workforce in childcare centres. If they are not available, how can we know what the current situation is or if there is progress in getting more men employed? Table 11.1 shows some statistics from six countries. Boys and girls in childcare centres in their younger years meet very few men, if any at all. When they grow older, the chances are higher, and in school and after-school care centres they are almost certain to meet a male employee. Childcare services continue to be one of the most 'gender-segregated' fields of work in the whole labour market. The younger the children, the fewer the men. Take Denmark for example. Only 59 male pedagogues are today working in 'vuggestuer' (for under-threes), supplemented by 293 non-trained assistants. In total 5 per cent of those employed are male, whereas in after-school care services the figure is 25 per cent. Moreover, Denmark has the world record in employing men in childcare centres!

Policies

To recruit male workers for the childcare services, and to keep them, demands that the following parties formulate an overall policy and action plan to carry this out:

Table 11.1 Male and female staff in services for children

	Total	Male %	Female %
Belgium–Flemish Community (1994)			
Kinderdagverblijf (centre for children 0–3)	2,806	1	99
Onthaalgezinnen (family day carer)			
in organized scheme	8,099	0.1	99.9
self employed	1,265	4	96
Denmark (1995)			
Vuggestuer (centre for children 0–3)			
paedagoger (trained)	3,333	2	98
assistants (untrained)	3,061	8	92
Total	6,394	5	95
Børnehaver (centre for children 3–6) and age-integrated centres			
paedagoger (trained)	16,578	6	94
assistants (untrained)	10,592	14	86
Total	27,170	9	91
Total (0–6)	–	8	92
Fritidshjem (centre providing care and recreation for school-aged children, aged 6–10)			
paedagoger (trained)	5,745	26	74
assistants (untrained)	3,405	24	76
Total	9,150	25	75
Finland (early 1990s)			
Nearly 4% of preschool teachers (working in centres for children aged 0–7) were men			
Spain			
Autonomous Community of Madrid			
Public services for children aged 0–3, 0–4, 0–6	1,076	8	92
City of Barcelona			
Centres for children aged 0–3	413	4	96
Sweden (1994)			
Daghem (centre for children 0–6)	71,311	3	97
Fritidshem (centre providing care and recreaton for school-aged children, aged 6–10)	19,570	16	84
United Kingdom (1991)			
In the Census, the occupational group 'childcare and related occupations' was the most gender-segregated occupation: over 98% of workers were female.			

Source: Jensen (1996)

- the state;
- local authorities;
- voluntary and private organizations;
- individual childcare centres;
- the training system;
- trade unions
- parents' organizations;
- careers advisors;
- employment agencies.

It is also important to establish a system that will monitor, evaluate and review developments in this field. Cooperation between these parties is vital to achieve the full effect.

It is in the individual centre that the policy and the action plan become reality by more men being appointed. When men are appointed, changes take place in the daily life of the centre. The centre can in all areas discuss the importance of having men employed.

Training institutions are the main places to promote the recruitment of men into childcare services. If qualified men cannot be found to fill positions, then there is no point in local authorities, organizations or individual childcare centres having fine ideas about employing more men, without any consequences. Therefore, entry into training is the key to getting more men into the profession. All in all, the training institutions can be the prime movers in recruiting more men into childcare services. They often have contacts with many individual childcare centres and with the authorities responsible for further training.

Other policies to encourage more men involve the provision of advice and support. In Finland, Norway and Great Britain, you will find examples of the formation of networks of male staff. Improvements in wages and employment conditions would be an important lever in raising the status of the job. This would improve the working conditions of many women, whilst attracting more men into the profession too.

More research needs to be conducted in this area, as almost nothing can be found on the relationship and interrelations between boys/girls and men/women in childcare services. In particular, there is no research based on observations and interviews with children about their behaviour and feelings towards male staff.

To find examples of good practice in Europe (or in the rest of the world if it comes to that) is difficult. Again the Nordic countries are a clear exception. The equal rights childcare centre in Gothenburg has already been mentioned, and other Swedish municipalities have taken different initiatives. The Swedish Social and Equal Rights Minister convened a seminar in 1993 on this subject (Socialdepartementet, 1993). In Finland some research has been carried out holding interviews with male pedagogues and 'Nalleklubber' ('Bears Clubs') have been established. In Denmark in 1994 all 32 training institutes for pedagogues launched a campaign 'Children also need men', where colourful posters and brochures were widely distributed, and the campaign received massive press coverage. This campaign has probably had a great influence, as in 1996 22 per cent of the new students were men. One training institute has set up a long pre-course for unemployed men. The Employment Office in one region launched a recruiting campaign together with the trade unions for pedagogical staff and the two training institutes in the region. The Government's Children's Committee also asked the Cross Minis-terial Children's Committee to prepare a discussion paper on how the balance between men and women can become more appropriate in child-ren's everyday life (Bonde and Carlson, 1997).

Furthermore, the Nordic Council of Ministers has had a project under its Equal Rights Programme – the Recruitment of Men for Public Child-care Services (Flising, 1997) – during which, among other things, a Nordic conference was held. At this conference, Erik Hauglund from the Child and Family Department in Norway produced the following charac-terization of four of the Nordic countries: Denmark does it, Sweden analyses it, Norway talks about it and Iceland thinks about it. Now, however, Norway leads the way in policy formulation with an action plan, which is a rare thing compared to the rest of the world.

In Britain, the climate of discussion is quite different, with the morbid suspicion of men in general as potential child abusers. Nevertheless, good examples are also to be found. However, the fear of abuse has generally become accepted in many places: a male worker should not have physical contact with the children, not sit with them on his lap, not change nappies alone, and not have night duty in the girls' departments of residential homes. One of the strategies is the witness strategy, where a woman is always present when a man changes a nappy. In job interviews men are asked about their sexuality. In a recent television programme about a divorced father, he said that he does not dare to have physical contact with his child, because he is afraid of being accused of abuse, and thereby have his custody taken away.

For the last 11 years, the Sheffield Children's Centre has employed just as many men as women. It not only provides a gender mix, but also provides anti-racist and multicultural provision. Eighty per cent of the staff employed are from black and other ethnic backgrounds. The staff offer 12 community languages to users. Male staff from a diverse range of cultural backgrounds provide a dual positive image of gender and race directly to children. Among other things, the centre operates a witnessing policy which means that no member of staff, female or male can change a child unless accompanied by another staff member. The National Men in Childcare Support Network in the UK is based at the Sheffield Children's Centre. The Centre also takes part in the Careers Guidance Programme in Sheffield in a 'Guess my Job' line up in schools. One of the male nursery teachers says:

> Those of us in non-traditional jobs have to give clues and the young people attempt to come up with the job. I've never had a group say what my job is yet. I am a six-foot four-inch eighteen-stone ex-miner. They can't visualize me working with young children. Every time I've told them what my job is they laugh without exception. I often pursue this and the stereotypes pour out of them. This is why I know that my work with children is so important particularly during the formative years when gender roles and attitudes are taking shape.

Pen Green Centre in England, which is a family centre, where a couple of men are employed, runs groups for fathers and discusses how fathers are received at the centre. This centre has been a partner in a project with Emilia-Romagna (Ghedini et al., 1995). Emilia-Romagna is a region in Northern Italy which has established many acclaimed childcare centres. The regional government collaborated with a number of local authorities to undertake a project about the role of fathers and how fathers can be better integrated into the life of the childcare centres. Part of the background to the project was that it would have taken many years to have employed more men in the centres, and they did not wait. A report on good practice in several European countries on how to involve fathers in the life of childcare centres has been published by the Centro di Cooperazione Familiare, a research institute in Rome (Cacaca and d'Andrea, 1996).

In Spain, as shown in Table 11.1, some municipalities have a high percentage of men employed. Some years ago, a centre in Valencia had employed an equal number of men and women, and men and women also took turns to be the head of the centre. However, now it is a 'normal' centre because of a shift in the political majority in the town council. Today some projects on this issue of recruiting more men are to be found in Murcia and Barcelona.

Everywhere, we see a dawning interest in getting more men employed. Both boys and girls are very happy to have men in the centres. Female staff are also pleased to have men working in the childcare services and find that staff cooperation improves. The parents, too, are pleased with men, and the men themselves like the job. So let us all get started.

Notes

1 A version of this article, in Danish, is published in: Leif Askland and Svein Ole Satagøen (eds) (1998), Menn I barnehargearbeid. Pedagogisk Forum, Norway.
2 It can be obtained free of charge from the European Commission Equal Opportunities Unit (DG V/A/3), 200 rue de la Loi, B-Bruxelles (in Danish, English, Flemish, French and Italian).

References

Bonde, H. and Carlsen, S. (1997), *Drenge i kvindedominerede miljøer. Det Tværministerielle Børneudvalg.*

Cacaca, M. and d'Andrea, L. (1996), *Fathers in Services for Young Children. Handbook in Good Practices in Sharing Responsibilities between Men and Women.* Rome: Centro di Cooperazione Familiare.

Carlquist, M.R. (1990), *Hela himlen. Ett jämstalldhetsprojekt i barnomsorgen.* Bromma, Bromma Municipality.

EC Childcare Network (1996a), The EC Childcare Network 1986-1996. A Decade of Achievements. Brussels.

— (1996b), *Quality Targets in Services for Young Children. Proposals for a Ten-Year Action Programme.* Brussels.

Flising, B. (1997), 'Rekrytering af män till offentlig barnomsorg', *TemaNord.* Nordiska Ministerrådet. København, 567.

Gade, K. and Larsen, K. (1997), *Pige-pædagogik.* Dansk Pœdagogisk Forum, Viborg.

Ghedini, P., Chandler, T., Whalley, M. and Moss, P. (1995), *Fathers, Nurseries and Childcare.* Brussels: European Commission Equal Opportunities Unit/EC Childcare Network

Granath-Sundqvist, E. (no date) *Framtidens daghem.* Gothenburg Municipality.

Hill, M. (1990), 'Involving men in the caring and educational services', *Local Government Policy-making, 17.*

Ruxton, S. (1992), *What's He Doing at the Family Centre? The Dilemmas of Men who Care for Children.* London: National Children's Home.

Socialdepartementet (1993) *Varför vill killar inte jobba på dagis och fritids?* Ett seminarium om män i barnomsorgen, Stockholm, February.

PART 4

Risks, allegations and protection: Does having more male workers increase the risks for young children and what can be done to protect children from risk and workers from false allegations?

12 Men as Workers in Services for Young Children

Svein Ole Sataøen
Sogn and Fjordane College, Sogndal, Norway

Background

First, I would like to say a few words about myself, and how I became interested in this particular issue. Since 1980, I've been working as a lecturer in education theory, and I have been doing research related to nursery schools.

On the basis of this work, I have developed a growing interest in men as workers in caring work; or to be more specific, men as workers in nursery schools. However, it took me ten years to approach this issue from a professional point of view. I have noticed, of course, the young men present in the lecture rooms. Nevertheless, I did not reflect on that specific situation of being male in a course of education overwhelmingly dominated by women and, further, consider a working life in an establishment where 93 per cent of the employees are women. So, it's interesting to notice the growing attention in Norway to men as carers, both as professionals and as fathers.

Today, I am involved in this field in several respects, including participating in a team working on 'Men in Nursery Schools', initiated by the Ministry of Children and Family Affairs. Our task was to produce some initial suggestions for initiatives to recruit and retain men as workers in nursery schools. That led to a plan of action, which appears as an Appendix to this chapter.

Additionally, together with a colleague, I am working on a collection of articles with the preliminary title, 'Men in Nursery Schools'. This collection will include both specialist articles and a portrayal of 15

Norwegian male workers in nursery schools. We aim to show variation and scope as regards men in caring functions, that is how old they are, where they come from (north/south/east/west, urban/rural areas, etc.), what positions they have, the size of the nursery school, how old the children are and so on. What roles do these men fulfil? Men as mountain climbers, cross-country-skiing with their own children, playing the guitar, men as actors on the stage?

Issues

This chapter is structured around the following questions.

- In the context of Norway wanting more male workers, is potential abuse by male workers seen as an issue? Are male workers seen as a risk?
- Have there been any cases of allegations against male workers? What happened and what were the consequences?
- Is there a discussion – in colleges or in government – about how to protect children from risk and workers (or students) from false allegations? Are there policies or practices for this purpose?
- If it is the case that the issue is less prominent in Norway (than in the UK for example), why is that?

I have tried to point to the positive aspects concerning male care and how it influences children's experiences in institutions. Consequently, men and sexual abuse is slightly outside of that on which I, as a researcher and lecturer, have decided to focus. This is not to imply that I have ignored these problems, but in my work so far I have not had the issue of men and abuse as a focal point.

In the context of Norway wanting more male workers, is potential abuse by male workers seen as an issue? Are male workers seen as a risk?

In short, this has hardly been a central issue in the discussions of men in nursery schools. The team working on initiatives for male recruitment in nursery schools made a conscious attempt to downplay that issue. Not because we do not regard it as important, but because so many others (i.e. the mass media) tend to exaggerate the topic. So, among other things, we focused on the problem of violence. In our opinion, to deal with this seriously – especially violence among boys – we have to start with a significant recruitment of men into children's everyday lives. There are many and complex explanations for the increasing violence in society. The absence of male role models is one factor to be taken into consideration. When presenting the nursery school profession to young men, it became urgent to highlight the aspect of care as quite the opposite of violence and destructiveness. The picture of caring men is (in this context) more in focus than the picture of men and violence or men as potential abusers. We wanted to describe men as people that you could trust, rather than raising spectres. As is well known, most sexual abuse takes place in the family, by fathers, but to get rid of fatherhood is by no means a solution.

Educational establishments have, of course, dealt seriously with the problem of sexual abuse, for instance in connection with students in teacher training practice. So far, I have not come across any case of sexual abuse in which students have been involved, and I have heard rumours about just one case. I will come back to how to keep children safeguarded against sexual abuse later in the chapter.

To my knowledge, people working in nursery schools are regarded with little or no suspicion by parents, colleagues or others. The male students will perhaps now and then experience a certain psychological strain when the media make such incidents front page news, for instance recent news coverage of a case in Wales. A questionnaire on this issue underlines the above statement. Students at Stord College distributed the questionnaire to male students and nursery school teachers. Nobody mentioned being under suspicion as a particular problem. Even so, some isolated incidents do occur, for example one male student who was a substitute in a nursery school (for a short period) was not allowed to help the five- to seven-year-old girls go to the toilet.

In order to create an awareness of these problems, nursery school teacher educators pay attention to specific subjects in the course of the three-year nursery school teacher education. At our college, we work with the theme 'Care for Children in Crisis' (Care for Vulnerable Children). We aim to enable the students to recognize signs of neglect and abuse. There are also on-going courses in nursery schools directed at meeting these problems; courses with headings such as 'Safe and Strong' and 'Know your own Body'. The children themselves are then trained to stand up for themselves, trained to be aware of what adults are allowed to do and not allowed to do in relation to children.

Have there been any cases of allegations against male workers? What happened and what were the consequences?

All European nations have one or more well-publicized cases of allegations. That goes for Norway, as well. Our case is the *Bjugn* case, named after the small village in which it took place. The exposure started in 1992 and went on until 1995. At one point, this case was said to be the worst sexual crime in Norway's history (*Dagbladet* (Daily News) 20 October 1992). It all started in March 1992 with a male assistant in a nursery school being suspected of having exposed himself indecently. The man was suspended and taken in for police interrogation. Then, on the 8 and 9 January, seven persons were taken in for interrogation. They were suspected of sexual abuse of 35 children altogether. Additionally, the assistant's wife, the local police sergeant, two other men and two women were taken into custody.

The police took 550 statements from 220 persons; there were 61 interrogations of 40 children; professionals detected, from investigations of 61 children, signs of sexual abuse in 31 children. Criminal charges were dropped against all except the male assistant. He was charged with the sexual abuse of ten children. The criminal case started in November 1993 and was completed in January 1994.

The man was acquitted on all counts, the defendant was paid damages as were the victims. There has been a political claim that there should be an investigation into the authorities' role in the case. We could say a lot in connection with this. Anyhow, this is a typical example of a case that goes off the tracks and then it is impossible to put it straight again. A journalist wrote a book entitled *What are we supposed to think?* in the aftermath of the case. She states in her conclusion that the *Bjugn* case has been an expensive one both for the police and the public health service. According to her, we shouldn't ask whether or not something happened in Bjugn, but rather look into why it was so difficult to reveal what was going on.

As in other countries that have had their own version of the *Bjugn* case, we noticed a subsequent marked decrease in reports to the police concerning children being subject to sexual abuse. Professionals hesitate and want to be more certain before they issue notification. Thus, the Bjugn legacy still frightens people.

Is there a discussion – in colleges or in government – about how to protect children from risk and workers (or students) from false allegations? Are there policies or practices for this purpose?
Yes, there is a discussion among professionals, and in the aftermath of the *Bjugn* case it has been reinforced. The Ministry of Children and Family Affairs presented a full consideration of this matter in a White Paper (No. 53 1992–93) on the sexual abuse of children. The National Assembly endorsed the proposal. The three main issues were:

- to strengthen the general knowledge in services, the police and the judicial system;
- to establish bodies which specialize in this field; and, among other things, to establish a national resource centre at Aker Hospital for sexually abused children;
- to increase children's legal protection and to safeguard against more abuse.

There is now a new law concerning nursery schools, including a number of paragraphs stating that persons who have been accused of or convicted of sexual abuse are not allowed to work in nursery schools. Consideration has also been given to introducing such restrictions on workers in other services for young children. The paragraphs in question (Regulation concerning Police Certificate) are to be found in Appendix 2. This is quite a strict code of laws; everybody is seen as a potential abuser. That means that everybody has to prove that his or her hands are clean. Furthermore, this will apply to students in their teaching practice.

There is always the danger of over-reaction, but how should we meet such a danger? Recently, a male student showed me an advertisement concerning employment in a nursery school situated far out in the countryside. The advert underlined the nursery school's particular focus on happiness and humour. The next sentence said that the applicant had to provide a satisfactory certificate showing that they had not been accused or convicted of sexual abuse. Quite a paradox, isn't it?

Another nursery school in one of the main Norwegian towns has stated explicitly that this year one of its aims was to bring to light sexual abuse of children – the poor children and poor parents.

The new set of laws concerns those (both men and women) who have a criminal record of sexual abuse. Staff who do not have a criminal record are the great challenge. Nevertheless, the new law is one step in a positive direction. It shows that everybody takes this seriously and that – in the aftermath of the *Bjugn* case – we will really work out the problem. Educational establishments might need to give greater attention to this issue (without knowing all the colleges in Norway in detail, I am nevertheless confident in saying that there is much that is still left to professional judgement in this area).

If it is the case that the issue is less prominent in Norway (than in the UK) why is that?

I do not know enough about English or other European nursery schools to conclude anything definite here. However, my impression is that there are more cases notified in England than, for instance, in Norway. This may be due to there actually being more cases in England or to the fact that the cases in question are more likely to be disclosed.

What I do know, is that the Norwegian nursery school organization and culture is a preventive measure in itself. Norwegian nursery schools are small, with few children and a large number of staff members; there are open areas and playgrounds; and parents have a say in the daily life of the nursery school. From the outset, it seems almost impossible to commit sexual abuse in a nursery school environment. Nevertheless, it does happen now and then. At the same time, we have to remember that the confident relationship established between adult and child in a nursery school environment might be exploited in contexts outside the nursery school – by being used to trustworthy adults, children are potentially subject to sexual abuse by other adults.

Finally, a confession or a concession. I lecture in education theory and social science. We cover many issues throughout the students' three years of education. The issue dealt with above is one of the most difficult – not least because I struggle myself to comprehend the abuse that is committed. I think that I understand many aspects of the human psyche, but this particular aspect I cannot grasp. Moreover, I hesitate to investigate it. Perhaps this attitude is the very obstacle to making the nursery school a safe place for children?

Taboos are shadowing sensible thoughts, stereotypes tend to be more real than complex human beings, and the borderline between necessary physical contact and the natural response and perverted behaviour is difficult enough to point to, let alone to talk about openly.

Appendix 1
A Plan of Action for Recruiting and Keeping Men in Kindergartens

Introduction

Background

The following proposal for a plan of action for recruiting men into work with children in kindergartens, and for retaining those who are already working there, is a result of the work of a committee appointed by the Norwegian Child and Family Department.

The committee was established on 24 April 1995, as a follow-up to the conference 'Men In Kindergartens', which had been held on 1–2 December 1994 in Stavanger. The committee members included:

- Lars Maanum, Steinbråten Kindergarten;
- Tommie Nilsen, Hauketo Kindergarten;
- Svein Ole Sataøen, Sogn and Fjordane College;
- Morten Halvorsen, Vest Agder County Supervisor;
- Leif Askland, Stord/Haugesund College.

The Committee has had four meetings, one of which was combined with a 'mini-hearing'.

Tasks for the Committee

The Committee was to develop a plan of action with suggestions for developmental initiatives within the area of 'men in kindergarten' in 1996. The plan of action was prepared using as its starting point the report of a conference that took place in Stavanger.

The plan of action had to contain suggestions for initiatives at different levels – central (departmental level), regional (county), local (municipality) and institutional (kindergarten and college).

The Committee was also to evaluate further use of the video by Tommie Nilsen and Lars Maanum. After this, the Department would be free to consider the use of the suggested initiatives.

The Committee has, through discussions, expanded the meaning of the tasks and connected this with an official thinking which legitimizes the assignment, namely to recruit men for work in kindergartens and to stimulate them towards a long career working with children. This understanding is expressed in various official documents. The Committee hopes to point to formulations in Ot. paper No. 29 (1994–95) 'On the law about changes to the law of 9 June 1978 No. 45 regarding equal opportunity for both sexes' and 'Framework for kindergartens'.

The reasoning behind the plan of action

Men in kindergartens: a question of equal opportunity
The recruitment of men in work of a caring nature is given legitimacy in many official documents, for example statements, plans for education and propositions. In Norway, equal opportunity between the sexes is a clearly stated societal objective. If this is to be more than idealistic visions, we know that children must be able to see equal opportunity in practice. This is the point of Ot. paper No. 29 (1994–1995: 4): 'An essential argument for getting more men into work of a caring nature is the long-term change in attitude that male role models in childcare will cause.'

Masculine care is also part of the content of kindergarten
Men as care-givers and pedagogues for young children is not a main objective in 'Framework for kindergartens' (NOU, 1992: 17). We can still interpret the analysis of children's conditions while growing up and becoming socialized described in the 'Framework for kindergartens' to mean that it would be impossible, according to the aims listed, to work

toward such goals without having both men and women working with the children.

Women have always been the ones who have worked out both form and content in the kindergarten. Over time, Norway has developed a kindergarten tradition of which it is proud. Most people agree that this tradition maintains a high level of quality. It is important to use this tradition as a starting point for the further development of kindergartens, and we think it important that men take more responsibility in affecting this development than they have done so far, both concerning form and content. Many men who start working in kindergartens meet a strong feminist culture in which it is hard for men to work. To find the special features of masculine care and make them part of the job description for men working in kindergartens is an important perspective in the proposed initiatives in this plan. This involves making men conscious of their responsibility and function in caring for children.

Sexual equality: a question of adapting views of sexual roles in both men and women

Both boys and girls have, throughout their adolescence, been exposed to a system of social control which forces them into traditional career choices based on their sex.

The women's movement has, through many years of work, been able to open doors in terms of education and careers for women, and to give girls aspiration to untraditional choices. On the men's side, there has not been a corresponding social movement to challenge the traditional sex roles. Therefore, it is uncommon for men to choose an education that will result in a traditional female occupation - and those who do seldom last for long in this kind of job.

Nowadays, there are more women applying for male-dominated careers than men applying for female-dominated careers. There are multiple reasons for this, but it is likely that the pressure of conformity is greater for men than for women. In other words, it is more socially acceptable for women to have male-dominated occupations than it is for men to have female-dominated occupations. Women who choose male-dominated work increase their social status by doing so. Men who choose female-dominated jobs lose social status. This background is important to consider when discussing initiatives to encourage men to choose untraditional education and careers.

Men must learn what their career opportunities are. Care-giving work, especially work in kindergartens, is an area with which men don't identify themselves. Those who begin working at kindergartens meet a dominant women's culture that many men don't want to be in, and they don't have the power to change. Kindergarten work is low-paid and has a low status. Changes in this area will not be made overnight. It is the long-term social changes which will have the greatest effect and these must take place over time.

Care is the opposite of violence
The attempt to encourage more men to work in kindergartens can be seen in the context of other societal objectives. We feel that it is important to look at education in the field of care providers in connection with a reduction in the rising crime rate in our society.

Social responsibility, care, love for others, and the ability to relate and have respect for others are common to all and are basic values in our society. Increased violence and other anti-social behaviours are a sign that today's society has a growing problem with transferring these values from generation to generation.

The explanations for the increase in violence in society are inseparable and complicated. The absence of male role models in the form of fathers or other visible male figures, is a partial explanation. In this regard, it is important to present care careers as a clear alternative for young boys who are beginning to think about a choosing a career.

Objectives

The group has worded the proposed plan of action according to the following goal: 'To find realistic measures for recruiting and keeping men who are suitable for working with children.'

Recruiting men to work in kindergartens involves both kindergarten teachers and assistants. To cooperate with both colleges that offer kindergarten teacher training, and upper secondary schools which offer kindergarten assistant training is, therefore, central and natural.

Short-term and long-term perspectives
The overall goal has both a long-term and a short-term perspective within the various initiatives in the action plan.

The short-term perspective
The action plan will cover recruitment initiatives and maintenance initiatives that can be put into practice at once. The target group for the short-term initiatives are men who are considering work with kindergarten children, and those who are already working in kindergartens.

The long-term perspective
Initiatives that are put into use now, with a short-term perspective, can also have a long-term effect. With this plan of action, we will also make suggestions for initiatives aimed at children and young people, in the hope of affecting their future opinions about care for young children, both as a future parent and with regards to future career choices. We will also suggest opinion-creating initiatives aimed at mothers and fathers of young children.

Assumptions that form the background for the plan of action

Qualifications
It is necessary to emphasize that there must be qualification requirements connected to every recruiting initiative. Adults (women and men) working in a kindergarten must take an interest in their work, and be willing to evolve professionally for the benefit of the children. Men working in the kindergarten must see the meaning in their developing the ability to:

- fulfil the child's need for warmth;
- see the child's need for mastering things;
- be grown-up in a way that the child can somehow identify with;
- recognize and fight for the child's ability;
- be grown-up persons in relation to the child's behaviour.

(From the booklet to the video *The Kindergarten – a workplace for men*, BFD, 1995.)

Salary and working conditions, equal opportunity

This is a question that lies beyond the mandate of this group, but we would like to point out that we feel it has great importance for the recruitment of men to work in kindergartens. Some of the main issues for the governmental department concerned, the central Union of Municipalities and the different working associations should be:

- salaries equal to those of teachers;
- salary adjustments according to the level of education;
- rewards for men and women who are directly involved in pedagogical work concerning the youngest children, for a longer time.

The group has not yet considered the question of quotas, as this has already been handled.

The construction of a plan of action

The plan of action is divided into several levels, depending on where they are supposed to start and who is responsible for bringing them to life.

- Level 1: The state
- Level 2: The county, for example Director of Education, Chief of County's Board of Education and County Doctor;
- Level 3: Municipalities;
- Level 4: Institutions, for example kindergartens, lower secondary schools and colleges.

The borders between the different levels can fluctuate. Most levels depend on the department as the initiator (see under 'Salary', above) The plan is split up into four main columns, in which each initiative is linked with a target group, and where it lists the content of the initiative and who has the chief responsibility for setting it into action. A summary of all of the initiatives can be found on the last page of the plan of action.

The group which has made suggestions for the plan of action defines itself as a participator in relation to some of the initiatives. In the plan, this group is referred to as the 'MIB group'.

Plan of action

Efforts linked with concrete recruiting (short-term perspective)
Level 1: The state

- Establish and train county contacts and a network in every county.
- Make materials for the recruitment campaign.
- The recruitment campaign.
- Establish educational programmes for men without a sufficient education so that they fulfil the requirements for acceptance into preschool educational studies.
- Establish a basic course and a first year upper secondary school course—child and youth work.
- Stimulate local development work linked with various problems related to men as pedagogues and care-givers.
- Create a booklet of ideas for kindergartens about how they can work together with fathers.
- Work on suggestions for a plan of action for colleges and universities.
- 'Men who work with children' – article gathering.
- Basic research on the theme of 'men as pedagogues', 'men as care-givers' and 'male care'.
- Stimulate development work in upper secondary school and colleges regarding students who have chosen untraditional careers (both women and men).
- Activate relevant organizations towards use of their organizational apparatus with regards to this plan of action.

- Take initiatives in informing the military and in the administration for conscientious objectors.
- Invite the relevant departments to a 'theme day', during which the plan of action is presented.

Level 2: The county

- Course for advisors in lower and upper secondary schools, and employment offices.
- Offer a study programme at the upper secondary level for working with children and young people. Distance learning in military camps and for conscientious objectors.
- Information stands at educational fairs for upper secondary schools and colleges.

Level 3: Municipalities

- Provide guidance on how the municipality can recruit and keep men working in kindergartens.
- Work on targets for advertising temporary job openings geared towards men who are waiting to enter military service.

Level 4: Institutions

- Action programmes for students who choose non-traditional careers.
- Establish contact and relationships between kindergartens and the employment exchange/personnel office.
- Set up networks for men working in kindergartens.

Efforts linked with men's general ability and need for the care of young children (long-term perspective)
Level 1: The state

- Evolve teaching aids for the compulsory lower secondary school linked with sexual roles and career choices.
- Evolve a package of courses for use in health centres and other institutions which have contact with parents/fathers.

Focus: Parental actions
'You're a father!'
• Appoint a committee which looks at soldiers' training from a care-related perspective.
• Offer work of a caring nature to the conscripts who wish this.

Level 2: The county

• Offer courses in connection with giving birth.

Level 3: Municipalities

• Establish discussion groups for men who are on paternity leave related to 'open days' in the kindergarten.
• Run experiments with 'open' kindergartens for fathers who are on paternity leave.

Level 4: Institutions

• Encourage experiments with compulsory care-giving practice in the Eighth Grade in the lower secondary school.
• Action programmes for the kindergartens' meeting and working with the fathers.

Appendix 2
Regulation Concerning Police Certificates

Section 1 Introductory provision

Whoever intends to work in a day care institution shall produce a satisfactory certificate from the police; see Section 20, first paragraph, of the Act. Under Section 20 of the Day Care Institutions Act 'satisfactory certificate' means a certificate showing whether the person has been accused of, indicted for or convicted of violations of the provisions of the General Civil Penal Code referred to in Section 3, second paragraph, of this regulation. A satisfactory certificate is a condition for appointment. The certificate shall not be more than three months old.

'Whoever intends to work in a day care institution' means all day care institution staff carrying out various tasks in the institution, persons holding long-term contracts, substitutes attached to a more established substitution arrangement and persons performing civilian work in lieu of military service.

When considering approval of a private day care institution the municipality shall, in cases where the owner him/herself intends to work in or for other reasons to be regularly present in the day care institution, verify that a satisfactory police certificate exists for the owner.

Section 2 Scope

All approved day care institutions are encompassed by this regulation.

Section 3 Content of the police certificate

The police certificate shall state whether the person has been accused of, indicted for or convicted of sexual abuse of children, see Section 20, first paragraph, of the Act.

'Sexual abuse of children' means violations of Sections 195, 196, 212 (first paragraph, subparagraph 3), and Section 212, second paragraph, of the General Civil Penal Code.

Impositions of fines, referrals to a municipal mediation board, waivers of prosecution and withdrawn charges and indictments shall not be stated in the certificate.

Section 4 Procedure

The employer shall in the text of the advertisement make applicants aware that a police certificate will be required upon appointment, but that it shall not be enclosed with the application. A certificate shall only be required of the applicant who is offered the position. A police certificate shall be available before the person takes up the position.

Act No. 52 of 11 June 1971 on Registration of Convictions and Regulation No. 4 of 20 December 1974 on Registration of Convictions apply to the issue of certificates, subject to the exclusions and specifications stated in Section 3 of this regulation.

Section 5 Treatment of police certificate

The police certificate shall be kept in a place inaccessible to unauthorized persons, and shall be destroyed immediately after being used in connection with appointment or for the purpose for which it was obtained, cf. Section 4 of the regulation.

Section 6 Duty of confidentiality

Whoever becomes aware of information through a police certificate is obliged to prevent unauthorized persons gaining access to or knowledge of such information. Violation may be punished under Section 121 of the General Civil Penal Code.

Section 7 Consequences of an unsatisfactory police certificate

If a person who is offered employment in the day care institution is unable to produce a satisfactory police certificate, the person in question may not work there.

The municipality may refuse to approve a day care institution if, after a police certificate is demanded in conformity with Section 20, third paragraph, of the Act, a police certificate is not produced or the certificate produced is not satisfactory.

13 Men as Childcare Workers: Are the Risks Worth the Benefits?

Susan J. Kelley

College of Health and Human Sciences, Georgia State University, Atlanta, GA

Introduction

Although the need to increase the number of men working as day care workers has been recognized in the United States since the 1970s, efforts to significantly increase the number of men working with young children have resulted in only minimal success. The need for male workers in childcare has become more critical with the changing demographics of the US family. Currently, one in every seven children in the United States is raised in a home without a father. Within the African-US population, it is estimated that one out of three children lives without a father present in the home. In low-income areas, especially in the inner cities, the incidence of father-absent homes is even higher. Tragically, many of these children have never met their fathers, and some do not even know their father's identity.

Numerous factors influence the number of men employed in childcare settings. A major factor, undoubtedly, is societal gender bias. Whereas women have made great strides in the last two decades in entering traditionally male-dominated professions such as law and medicine, significant numbers of men have failed to enter traditionally female-dominated professions such as nursing and early childhood education. Thus, some of the traditionally female-dominated professions have actually suffered as the result of the so-called 'women's movement' due to the fact that intelligent women now have more professional opportunities and, therefore, are opting for better paid and more prestigious careers. Unfortunately, the combination of low pay and low status associated with early childhood education works against attracting men into the field.

Gender bias is also evident when a parent, or day care director, suspects that men who choose to work with children, must be gay. It is also likely that our society has become more homophobic than ever about men as workers in day care due to parental fear, albeit unwarranted, that children could contract HIV from a gay, male worker. Even the most highly educated individuals loose their objectivity due to the tremendous fear associated with AIDS. Homophobics also fear that gay men are likely to sexually abuse children in their care.

Another factor negatively influencing the inclusion of men in early childhood education is the fear that men are at greater risk than women of sexually abusing children in their care. This chapter will address the issue of child sexual abuse in day care, with emphasis on the aspects of the problem that have implications for men as workers in services for young children.

Abuse of children in day care centres

The increased number of children attending day care, combined with heightened awareness of sexual abuse of children, has resulted in a rise in the number of reports of sexual abuse in day care settings. Such reports typically receive much more media attention than cases of intra-familial abuse, leading to the perception that children are at increased risk of being sexually abused in day care. Several myths have resulted from media attention and societal biases.

Myth 1 Children who attend day care are at increased risk of sexual abuse

Results of a large incidence study of abuse in day care settings conducted in the United States by Finkelhor, Williams and Burns (1988) indicate that children have a greater chance of being abused at home than in a day care setting. In fact, children under the age of six are almost twice as likely to be abused in their own home as they are in a day care centre.

Myth 2 Gay workers will molest children in their care
The available research indicates that children are more likely to be sexually abused by a heterosexual married man, than by a man who is gay. Homosexuals should not be confused with paedophiles. Paedophiles are sexually attracted to children exclusively, with no sexual interest in adults, whereas homosexuals are attracted to individuals their age and gender. However, a paedophile could be sexually attracted to a child of the same gender and would be referred to as a same-gender paedophile, not a homosexual.

Myth 3 Excluding men from in positions that involve direct care for young children in day care will prevent abuse in day care
Slightly less than half of the offenders are direct care providers. Teachers comprised 30 per cent of the offenders and teachers' aides, 15 per cent. The remaining 55 per cent were relatives of staff (25 per cent); owners and directors (16 per cent); non-childcare staff (8 per cent); and outsiders (5 per cent). Given that direct care providers represent less than half of offenders, policies to protect children must address all individuals who could have access to children.

Myth 4 Sexual abuse in day care is committed almost exclusively by men
Although, in general, women commit fewer sex offences against children than men do, the proportion of women involved in day care abuse cases is considerably higher than in cases of intra-familial abuse. More specifically, it is estimated that women are perpetrators in 5–10 per cent of all child sexual abuse cases. In the study by Finkelhor, Williams and Burns (1988) of 260 cases of day care abuse, 40 per cent of offenders were female; in Faller's (1988) sample, 50 per cent were female; and in Kelley's (1989) sample, 55 per cent were female. In these studies, women abused both male and female students. Thus, parents and employers must keep an open mind with regard to females as perpetrators in day care settings. Policies to protect children from abuse must be developed with both men and women in mind.

In the study by Finkelhor, Williams and Burns (1988), women were more likely to be involved in multiple-perpetrator, multiple-victim cases; they were more likely than men to have abused over a period of time; and were more likely to be direct care providers, as opposed to ancillary workers or relatives or friends of workers. Women were more likely than men to commit multiple sexual acts and more likely to commit acts involving penetration. They were also more likely than men to use physical force, threats and intimidation.

Another way to look at the gender issue is that given the very small number of males working in day care settings in the United States, they commit a disproportionate amount of sexual abuse. Nonetheless, great attention needs to be paid to understanding female workers as abusers.

Myth 5 Sexual abuse of young children is usually limited to touching and fondling

Table 13.1 lists the types of sexual abuse reported in the four day care studies conducted in the United States. The sexual acts reported range in severity from fondling to intercourse. It can be noted that while fondling is the sexual act reported most often, highly intrusive sexual acts involving penetration are frequently reported.

Penetration of the anus or vagina with a foreign object is commonly reported by children abused in day care. Foreign objects reported include pencils, needles, knives, scissors and sticks. In some instances the perpetrator will distort the child's perception of what is being placed inside their vagina or rectum, as in the case example below.

It can be seen in Table 13.1 that children often reported being forced to engage in sexual acts with other children. Forcing children to sexually abuse other children can cause them to view themselves as perpetrators instead of victims, often resulting in intense feelings of guilt.

A disturbing number of children in each of the studies reported sexual exploitation involving pornography. When children in day care centre cases report having pornographic photographs or videos taken, the pornography is typically not recovered by law enforcement. As a delay from children's first disclosures to police involvement is typical, lack of

Table 13.1 Types of abuse in four studies (%)

	Faller (1988)	Finkelhor, Williams and Burns (1988)	Kelley (1989)	Waterman *et al.* (1993)
Sexual abuse/any type	100	100	100	100
Fondling of genitals	67	71	92	89
Digital penetration	NR	29	80	89
Oral genital sex	71	30	74	65
Vaginal intercourse	54	12	51	40
Rectal intercourse	54	14	49	33
Foreign object penetration	NR	15	64	51
Pornography	NR	14	74	37
Sexual acts among children	74	15	70	NR
Physical abuse	NR	31	85	64
Threats/terrorizing acts	13	13	52	80
Ritualistic abuse	13	13	52	80

NR = Data not reported.

physical evidence may be the result of offenders hiding or destroying the pornography once they learn they are under suspicion. Another possible explanation for lack of physical evidence is that, in some instances, cameras are used as part of a "game" to get the children to participate in sexual acts while pretending to be television or movie stars rather than to produce pornography for commercial purposes or private use. For example, children in several day care centre cases reported play the 'naked movie star game' during which sexual abuse occurred.

Offenders

Motivation
Faller (1990) has developed a typology for the reasons adults sexually abuse children in day care and divides them into two general categories: first, unplanned sex with children, and, second, planned sex with children. This information is useful in planning policies to protect children.

Unplanned sexual abuse

Unplanned sexual abuse comprises three categories. The first, circumstantial sexual abuse, involves a perpetrator with no past history of sexual activity with children who, because of physical or life circumstances, engages in sex with a child. Physical circumstances include experiencing sexual arousal as a result of physical contact with the child or viewing the child's genitals. Other circumstances that are thought to lead to sexual abuse of children in day care are the absence of other sexual outlets or some life stress resulting in regression.

The next category, naive paedophiliac abuse, refers to persons with paedophiliac tendencies who are initially unaware of them. Often they feel an affinity for children that is, at the onset, unrelated to sexual attraction. It is only after they work closely with children, such as in a day care settings, that they experience sexual attraction to them.

The third category of unplanned sexual contact with children involves what Faller (1990) has termed 'induced sexual abuse'. This involves offenders who sexually abuse in day care who have no intention of doing so but who are manipulated or coerced into sexual abuse by other offenders who play leadership roles. Offenders who are induced to abuse in day care tend to be women.

Planned sexual abuse

Faller (1990) has identified four types of planned sexual abuse in day care:

- calculated paedophiliac abuse;
- entrepreneurial sexual abuse;
- sexual maltreatment by child haters;
- ritualistic abuse.

Calculated paedophiliac abuse involves abusers whose primary sexual orientation is towards children. They tend to abuse more than one child and consciously choose to work where they have easy access to children. Day care may be a particularly attractive setting for these offenders because the victims are young, pliable, and less likely than older children to make coherent and convincing statements in a court of law.

The second category, entrepreneurial abuse, is motivated by profit and typically involves reports of production of pornography and child prostitution. Strangers may be brought to the day care centre to have sex with children. In addition, children often report being removed from the centre and taken to unfamiliar places where they are sexually abused by strangers.

The third category, sexual abuse by people who hate children, involves offenders who wish to cause great psychological and sometimes physical harm to children (Faller, 1990). Acts of child-hating abusers tend to be sadistic.

The last category described by Faller (1990) is ritualistic abuse, which she describes as limited to situations where sexual abuse is part of some rite that appears to have significance related to a type of religion, Satanism, witchcraft or other cult practice. As can be noted in Table 13.1, each of the four studies included allegations of ritualistic abuse.

Policies to protect children and staff in day care settings

Unfortunately, research findings have been unable to identify precautions that will preclude sexual abuse from occurring in day care settings. However, certain precautions can be taken to decrease the risk. Unlimited parental access to day care facilities is one of the few factors that has been found to decrease the risk of sexual abuse (Finkelhor, Williams and Burns, 1988). Therefore, policies should encourage parental visits at any time, without a requirement of prior notification.

Although screening workers for past records of sexual offences and other criminal acts is important, most checks will come up negative. Thus, day care facilities cannot rely on protecting children simply by conducting checks on criminal records. Equally important is screening day care staff for a broad range of background information, including prior work history and emotional problems.

Primary prevention programmes aimed at teaching children about general safety issues, including sexual abuse, should be implemented, but not viewed as a panacea. Some of the most positive aspects of these prevention programmes is teaching children not to keep secrets from their parents and to report abuse to a trusted adult. Critics of these programmes believe they are ineffective in preventing abuse and only lead to increased feelings of guilt when abuse does occur because in most situations, children are unable to thwart the adult's sexual acts. It appears that prevention programmes are less effective in primary prevention, that is preventing the abuse in the first place, and more effective in secondary prevention, that is in identifying past or on-going cases of child sexual abuse.

Measures to protect children from abuse may also protect staff from false allegations. As many allegations of sexual abuse in day care take place around toileting activities, day care facilities should minimize areas where staff can have total privacy with children. This can be achieved by removing partitions in bathrooms. Policies regarding who can take children to the toilet or be with them alone need to be established.

Conclusions

Numerous societal factors in the united States discourage the role of men in working with young children in childcare settings. These include low wages, low status, gender biases against men working in 'caring' professions and homophobia. Research findings clearly indicate that men are more likely than women to sexually abuse children in any setting, whether it be in home or day care. We also know that children are more likely to be abused in the home than in a childcare setting. Yet, banning men from all homes in which children reside is never debated. Discouraging or prohibiting men from working in childcare will not stop the sexual abuse of children, it will only serve to deprive children of diverse role models. We must determine what risk-benefit ratio we are willing to accept in all settings, and not single out childcare.

References

Faller, K.C. (1988), 'The spectrum of sexual abuse in day care: an exploratory study', *Journal of Family Violence*, *3*(4), 283–298.
— (1990), 'Sexual abuse in day care'. In: *Understanding Child Sexual Maltreatment.*

Newbury Park, CA: Sage, 191–210.

Finkelhor, D. and Kendall-Tackett, K. (1993), 'Epilogue: the research perspective'. In: J. Waterman, R.J. Kelly, M.K. Oliveri and J. McCord (eds), *Behind the Playground Walls: Sexual Abuse in Preschools*. New York: Guilford, 278–283.

Kelley, S.J. (1986), 'Learned helplessness in the sexually abused child', *Issues in Comprehensive Pediatric Nursing*, 9, 193–207.

— (1989), 'Stress responses of children to sexual abuse and ritualistic abuse in day care centres', *Journal of Interpersonal Violence*, 4(4), 502–513.

Waterman, J., Kelly, R.J., Oliveri, M.K. and McCord, J. (1993), *Behind the Playground Walls: Sexual Abuse in Preschools*. New York: Guilford.

14 Men as Workers in Professional Childcare Settings: An Anti-oppressive Practice Framework

Keith Pringle
Reader in Social Policy, University of Sunderland

Introduction

There is a current tension within British childcare discourse (both academic and practice-based), which I believe extends to the situation in other countries. At the same time as an emphasis on the importance of men in professional childcare is growing ever more clear, some commentators are pointing out that an uncritical advocacy of men's involvement in childcare entails considerable problems. Using data and experience primarily from the United Kingdom, I want to examine this tension and to suggest that, even though complete resolution may be unlikely, some creative and positive outcomes are possible.

Men engaged in childcare professionally have a major responsibility and opportunity to challenge the many negative attitudes and practices pervading our society which, I believe, are associated with some dominant forms of masculinity. Those dominant forms reflect the complex interplay of a range of sources of oppression, including heterosexism, racism, disablism, ageism and classism, as well as issues of gender. Thus, the project I am advocating here for men engaged in childcare is broad in its anti-oppressive scope. However, at its heart remains the central objective of challenging men's violence (Pringle, 1995).

It can be argued there are concerns about formal childcare settings which are more pressing than those in the context of 'home' care. First, where people entrust their children to 'out of home' childcare services for whatever reason, it may well be that they should expect those children to be at least as safe (perhaps even safer) than when they are in their own homes. Therefore, observable standards of welfare and safety are required in particular in such settings. Second, and this links with my first point, 'out of home' childcare settings often cater for a larger number of children, one way or another, than many 'in home' settings. As a result, a lack of welfare or safety in such settings may have negative consequences for much larger numbers of children. There seems no doubt from British and US experience that, for this very reason, perpetrators of sexual abuse may actually target jobs in childcare to gain multiple access to children. Once again, standards of welfare and safety are at a particular premium in these environments. Thus an argument can be constructed for taking particularly rigorous action to promote children's welfare in 'out of home' situations.

Increasing men's participation in childcare practice

Much support for men's greater inclusion in professional childcare (and at home) has come from the European Commission which, in its 1992 Recommendation (EC, 1992 – 92/241/EEC, Article 6) makes clear that member states should promote and encourage increased participation by men for the care and upbringing of children. The 1994 White Paper on European social policy (EC, 1994), re-emphasizes the importance of this theme. The EC Network on Childcare has also carried it forward with great energy (EC Network on Childcare, 1993 and 1996; and Jensen, 1996), albeit with very little concrete impact on the British government (Moss, 1994) (although this may now change following the New Labour government's enthusiasm for the Social Chapter). The Network in many of its publications (e.g. EC Network on Childcare, 1993; and Jensen, 1996) recognizes the need for greater inclusion of men in formal childcare services such as nurseries and family centres and sees men working in those settings as being able to promote men's greater participation in the home care of children.

In Britain a series of documents and articles have also advocated more inclusion of men in statutory and non-statutory services for children (Ruxton, 1991; Holt, 1992; and Chandler, 1993). Many of these contributions focus particularly on men working in family centres.

This chapter summarizes the main arguments for men's greater participation in formal childcare settings advocated by the Childcare Network and the British commentators mentioned above. At the same time, a critique of these arguments will demonstrate my central premise: that the undoubted advantages of men's greater participation in formal childcare settings can only be gained if men's practices in this field are grounded in a broad anti-oppressive framework placing the issue of men's power centre-stage.

Men's greater participation in childcare: a constructive critique

The main arguments in favour of men's greater participation in formal childcare settings seem to be as follows.

• It will benefit children (both boys and girls) by providing them with positive male role models who are important for their identity formation and to help them realize that some men are safe; meeting their need to be held and receive physical contact from men (Chandler, 1994).

• It will benefit women by relieving them of part of the responsibility for childcare, which in turn may help to equalize power relations (Thompson, 1995). In specific relation to the family, it will allow women easier participation in the labour market and give them more choice (EC Network on Childcare, 1993), thereby breaking down gender stereotypes in society.

• It will benefit men by allowing them to enjoy childcare if that is what they want to engage in (EC Network on Childcare, 1993; and Chandler, 1994); helping them to redefine their identities as men (EC Network on Childcare, 1993: 12), by developing those aspects of themselves relating to nurturance and connectedness.

I now want to critically review these arguments one by one. My main contention is that while there is much of value in these arguments, two qualifications need to be added: first, their analysis is over-simplistic for a variety of reasons; and, second, the value they promise can only be achieved by placing men's greater childcare engagement within a broad model of men's practices – a model which centres on issues of men's power and is grounded in the materiality of children's, women's and men's lived experience.

The benefits to children
Much research has demonstrated that, generally speaking, men can perform parenting perfectly adequately. The problem is that for various structural and/or personal reasons many men choose not to fulfil that potential or to fulfil it only in a selective or partial way (Segal, 1990: 37–46; and Marsiglio, 1995). That men on the whole can indeed provide successful nurturance to children is borne out by more recent research in Britain (Barker, 1994) and the United States (Marsiglio, 1995). More-over, there is every reason to believe that the potential capacity of men to nurture is also applicable to those who work in more formal childcare settings (Ruxton, 1991; and Chandler, 1993).

However, the analysis of men as childcarers becomes over-simplistic when claims are made that men's presence in formal and informal settings is a necessity. We can begin to deconstruct such deterministic claims by referring to studies on the developmental progress of children in lesbian households (e.g. Golombok, Spencer and Rutter, 1983; and Patterson, 1992). No-one would deny that more research on this issue is required to broaden the evidence and to deepen it longitudinally. However, there is an impressive consistency in the data we do possess: the children in these households seem to develop emotionally and physically just as well as children brought up in heterosexual ones.

We are also increasingly aware that as children develop into adults, the processes by which they shape their identities are far from simple. A theme which sometimes occurs in advocacy of men being engaged in childcare is that boys will not be able to learn how to be fathers them-selves unless they too have father role models. While one would not deny that children may well benefit from emotional proximity to adults of both genders, there is a danger of being too crude and prescriptive in analysing this. For instance, it is increasingly apparent from research in the United States (Daly, 1995) and in the UK (Heward, 1996; and Pringle, 1997c) that men's construction of their masculinity, and in particular those aspects related to fatherhood, are heavily influenced in complex ways by significant female figures, not least mothers.

One can add to this sophisticated perspective the conclusions of feminist and pro-feminist analyses of the alleged need for a male figure at the centre of children's (and in particular boys') lives (Phillips, 1993: 143–198; and Pringle, 1995: 60–77). The same logic can be applied to the alleged necessity for men's presence in more formalized childcare provision (Jensen, 1996). Of course, many men will have much to offer as workers in childcare services. However, there seems to be no valid argument to support the contention that male workers must always be present in more formal childcare settings for the benefit of children (Pringle, 1992, and 1993).

So far in reviewing this debate, we have dwelt on the extent to which men's positive contributions to childcare are essential to children's welfare. It is time to introduce another vital and highly contentious factor into the argument, namely the violence of some men towards children.

In fact, many commentators fail to sufficiently take into account the potential 'down-side' of men's presence in childcare. For instance, the EC Network on Childcare, in strongly advocating men's greater participation mentions that 'taking more responsibility for children must also involve men taking more responsibility in other areas ... . They must acknowledge, take responsibility for and deal with negative male behaviour – family violence and abuse, sexual harassment, etc.' (1993: 14). However, this important theme is not expanded on and it sits within a text which otherwise largely details the virtues of men as carers of children. Similarly, Jensen (1996: 23), whose whole focus is the issue of men working in childcare services, devotes only one-and-a-half pages to the topic of men and sexual abuse in a document which is 55 pages long.

Whilst not denying the abuse of power which women may exercise over children (Hanks and Saradjian, 1991; Elliott, 1993; and Kelly, 1991 and 1996), men's violence presents a considerably larger threat in many respects. This is particularly true in relation to sexual violence (Pringle, 1995: Chapter 8) and, as we shall see, there is no reason to believe that this state of affairs is any different in terms of welfare settings.

There is considerable evidence, largely from the United States, that sexual abuse of children by welfare professionals may be at worrying levels (McFadden, 1984; Finkelhor, Williams and Burns, 1988; Fanshel, 1990; McFadden and Ryan, 1991; Margolin, 1991 and 1993; and Benedict et al., 1994). Foster care, nursery care, day care and residential care have been the areas subject to most statistical scrutiny.

In Britain, the plethora of major sexual abuse scandals making the headlines in the media have related to residential care and to some extent nursery care. However, there is no reason to believe that the other areas mentioned above will be any safer than residential or nursery care. On the contrary, some of them, especially foster care, offer an even greater degree of intimacy and isolation to potential abusers (Pringle, 1993a).

Following numerous 'scandals' relating to abuse in welfare settings, various strategies have been adopted by welfare agencies over the years to counter this danger. The fact that these scandals have continued and the resulting enquiry reports have replicated themselves, indicates those strategies may well be ineffective. However, let us consider them in a little more detail. Elsewhere I have examined these issues in depth (Pringle, 1992 and 1993). Here I will mention only four of the existing strategies to illustrate their limitations.

The first strategy is police checks and social services checks on job applicants (HMSO, 1992). Of course these should always be carried out because they may pick out a few abusers who have a record of some sort. However, we know from massive prevalence survey results (Finkelhor et al., 1990; and Kelly, Regan and Burton, 1991) that the vast majority of sexual abusers never come to the attention of any authorities whatsoever, let alone have a record. So checks on job applicants will only deal with a tiny fraction of abusers.

The second strategy is greater supervision of staff. This is advocated by both the Hunt Report (Hunt, 1994) and other commentators (Ruxton, 1991). Once again this may have value, but it is only limited. We know that a skilled perpetrator seems capable of abusing very young children even when there are staff in the same room. The Hunt Report (Hunt, 1994) itself acknowledges this.

The third strategy is the idea of using psychological tests or interviewing techniques to 'weed out' potential abusers. The Warner Report (HMSO, 1992) which was set up by the British Government specifically to look at the issue of abuse perpetrated by welfare personnel, reviewed the research on psychological profiling and concluded that no such profiling could effectively screen for abusers and potential abusers. The Report did advocate the use of close questioning of applicants at interview about their sexuality. Nevertheless, it is hard to see how this could screen for determined perpetrators, given research from work with perpetrators demonstrating the degree of sophistication that many adopt in getting close to children.

My fourth example of a limited strategy is the idea of training other staff to recognize signs of abuse occurring. Apart from being *'post hoc'* and, therefore, clearly unsatisfactory, this strategy (though worth carrying out) is unhelpful on a number of grounds: we know how hard it is to believe that trusted colleagues may be abusers; we also know the skill with which abusers 'cover their tracks' by scaring children about the outcomes of disclosures; finally, we know how hard it is for children to disclose or hint at abuse – particularly about people who have formal power over them.

If one reads the Warner Report (HMSO, 1992) what is striking is that it never even mentions the issue of the gender of perpetrators. This is surely odd simply in terms of the fact that, as was noted above, plentiful research indicates men and boys predominate as perpetrators of sexual abuse as a whole in society. Moreover, if we make allowance for the small numbers of men working in some areas of welfare, then there is very clear evidence (again almost all from the United States) that men account for a very large proportion of sexual abuse in fields as diverse as foster care, residential care, nursery care and day care (Finkelhor, Williams and Burns, 1988; Fanshel, 1990; Nunno and Rindfleisch, 1991; Rosenthal et al., 1991; Margolin, 1991 and 1993; and Ryan, McFadden and Wiencek, 1988).

At this point, I want to emphasize that I have not introduced the question of men's violence towards children within welfare settings in order to argue against men's presence in the provision of childcare. On the contrary, I accept that men can often provide a useful service to children. This discussion is offered in order to point out that men's potentially positive contribution has to be framed within a set of practices which guard against the negative impact (including abuse) which some men may have on the welfare of children. Later in this chapter, I will outline a gender-based strategy for limiting the scope of potential abuse by men in professional childcare. Of course, such a strategy will not stop abuse by women in childcare; other strategies are needed for that. I want to stress again that all the evidence suggests men are proportionately the predominant perpetrators of sexual abuse inside and outside welfare settings. I do not claim that my strategy will stop all abuse by men. However, it seems to me that it ought to be far more effective than the other strategies I critiqued above which have proven to be largely unhelpful.

The benefits to women
There is considerable validity in these arguments. For instance, Thompson (1995: 471) is no doubt correct in regarding men's greater involvement in child rearing and the consequent erosion of gender stereotyping around 'caring' as, at one level, a potential move towards social justice. However, when taken in isolation from other measures, this kind of approach can become over-simplistic.

It is not at all clear whether or not men's shift to childcare functions would necessarily result in benefits to women. For such benefits to occur, the wider social contexts in which that shift takes place must also be the object of positive anti-oppressive change. For instance, Hilary Graham (1983 and 1993) has explored the ways in which caring has come profoundly to underwrite many women's sense of self-identity and self-worth in the same way as achieving goals for oneself may play a major role in underwriting the self-identity of many men (Baldwin and Twigg, 1991). It may be that if some gender shift in childcare is to be attained, then more alternative ways of achieving self-identity and self-worth for women also need to be developed. If more men do enter childcare work, there is every indication at present, given the gender profile of social work management (Grimwood and Popplestone, 1993; and Pringle, 1995: 18–29, 191), that one major result will be more men occupying management posts in that sector. Consequently, the entry of more men to the childcare sector has to be accompanied by strategies to change the gendered power relations both inside welfare organizations themselves and in wider society. If men are serious about challenging those relations of power which are oppressive to women, then greater participation in childcare by them must occur within the framework of much broader anti-oppressive practices, including strategies by which men find more positive ways of expressing themselves in the lived experience of their relations with women, children and other men.

The benefits to men

Research on men as carers of children makes it clear that many men do enjoy that activity (Ruxton, 1991). I am not suggesting that men should be deprived of the opportunity to gain that satisfaction. However, the above discussion clearly indicates that men's right to this form of activity has to be balanced against the needs of both children and women.

This seems an appropriate point at which to highlight once again a particularly contentious issue. How can men's involvement in childcare within formal settings be combined with a policy that maximizes the safety of children – bearing in mind what was said at the very beginning of this chapter about the special urgency regarding safety in formal childcare settings? One very particular context for this concern which has already been addressed is the clear preponderance, proportionately, of men as perpetrators of sexual violence against children.

Earlier in this chapter, I promised that I would mention a strategy, based on my gender analysis, for increasing the safety of children from sexual abuse in situations where men are working as professional carers. Elsewhere (Pringle, 1995: 185–192) I have discussed that strategy at length; here I will summarize it. The strategy centres on a spectrum of adaptations to men's professional practice. Different forms of adaptation will be appropriate to different welfare situations: each welfare situation will be unique and must be looked at individually to assess the degree of potential risk to children in that specific setting.

Many of these adaptations to men's practice will be relatively small (e.g. male workers avoiding touch as far as possible in communicating with children). At the other extreme, there may be situations where one would contemplate asking men not to participate in some childcare work. However, I want to make very clear that I believe the number of occasions where that extreme approach is required will be very small indeed. The vast majority of adaptations will be at the minor end of the spectrum or somewhere in the middle (e.g. the idea of male staff co-working with female colleagues).

Clearly, in making the assessment of what degree of adaptation is required for each welfare situation, the criteria by which that assessment is made will be crucially important. I have also set out an initial framework for such criteria (Pringle, 1995: 187–18) and I summarize that here too. The more a particular setting has to take into account the criteria outlined in the list which follows, the more extensive may need to be the adaptations made by male staff there to the way they work.

- What is the age of the children here and how will that impact on their ability to say or show if they feel discomfort or abuse?
- What is the children's developmental level and what effect does that have in those same respects?
- Are there other issues which might make it harder for children to express discomfort or abuse in a specific setting, such as some physical disabilities?
- Are there reasons for thinking more children in this setting might have a history of sexual abuse?
- What level of physical and/or emotional intimacy with children by staff is required in this setting?
- What level of staffing is available here to make children feel more secure?
- Above all, what are the children in this setting telling us (in words and/or actions if they can) about what would make them feel safe?

It needs to be borne in mind that these are only preliminary sugges-tions. It may well be that a debate about appropriate criteria would be a useful development in helping us move forward.

It is important to add that such strategies will have a protective function not only for children but also for staff. I say this not because I believe it is common for children to make deliberate, false allegations of sexual abuse – it is, in fact, relatively rare. However, it may be more frequent for children who have already endured sexual abuse at some other time in their lives to genuinely misinterpret the actions of staff as having an abusive purpose. Often this will be due to the patterns of 'grooming' that abusers may have imposed on them in the past. So, I argue, protection is also afforded to staff by the strategies put forward here primarily for the safety of children.

The direct danger of sexual abuse to children is not the only issue relevant to the question of limitations on men's practice in this field. I and two colleagues have carried out a research project in the north-east of England comparing statutory services available to child and adult survivors of sexual abuse with those services preferred by service users (Gray, Higgs and Pringle, 1996 and 1997). One interesting set of findings related to users' preferences regarding who should provide them with therapy. The issue of gender figured very prominently (Gray, Higgs and Pringle, 1996: 194). The vast majority of users in our survey indicated a clear preference for women therapists; a minority expressed no prefer-ence either way; no-one expressed a preference for a man. The preference for women extended to male respondents and included the small minority who had been abused jointly by a man and a woman. No respondents re-ported sexual abuse perpetrated by a lone female. I would not, of course, consider drawing any firm conclusions from this one piece of research. Nevertheless, it adds material to the debate about how far we unreser-vedly accede to men's desire to work across the whole range of child welfare settings.

I now want to discuss another reason which is put forward for sug-gesting men's greater engagement in childcare will be of benefit to men themselves. As noted above, it is sometimes argued that such a move will assist men to positively re-create the way they express themselves as men. In other words, nurturing children may be a central route by which men re-evaluate their general behaviour, as men, in their dealings with other people. I do not discount the general idea behind this argument (Pringle, 1995: 209). However, I believe we have to be realistic and recognize that change in one particular aspect of a man's life, no matter how central, is unlikely to have an on-going and extensive impact on his overall behaviour, unless it becomes part of a wider anti-oppressive approach to the social world. In other words, we are once again appealing to the need for men to take positive action to change oppressive power relations within a broad practice framework if the benefits which engagement in childcare work is alleged to bring are to be realized.

This, of course, complements the conclusions I drew in the two earlier sections on benefits to children and to women. My central argument is that men's more extensive engagement in childcare activities, formally and informally, may indeed offer potential benefits to children, women and men themselves, but only if that engagement is set in a wider context of men's anti-oppressive practice. This involves men challenging dominant relations of power in the family, welfare services and society more generally. If such a broader practice is not implemented, then men's greater engagement in childcare by itself may simply result in replication of oppressive power relations in one form or another: annexation or colonization of initiatives developed by/for women; diversion of resources away from other initiatives promoting the well-being of women and/or children; perhaps even abuse of women and/or children (Pringle, 1995: 214–218). This seems an appropriate point at which to outline the form of such a comprehensive practice framework for men.

Challenging oppressive gender power relations: a practice framework for men

This final section briefly summarizes my previous work in delineating the principles of a framework for men's anti-oppressive welfare practice more generally (Pringle, 1995: 204–219). I refer readers to that previous work as it is impossible in the space available to do justice to the framework. I want to focus here on one element within the framework, adapted for specific application to childcare. This is an outline of what I have referred to elsewhere (Pringle, 1997a) as the 'domains of action' at which men's anti-oppressive practice has to take place. It is important to emphasize that these domains of potential action are applicable to all men seeking greater involvement in childcare across the whole spectrum of settings.

- Work with, and on, one's own personal and political oppressive behaviour in order to challenge it. One obvious example could be that men who may abuse children need to challenge their propensity to do so, otherwise their entry into childcare will seriously oppress, rather than benefit, children.
- Individual work with other men or boys to promote mutual challenge of oppressive behaviours. For instance, if more men enter into paid work at family centres and nurseries, it is possible that this could lead to more sexual exploitation of the women working there, unless men challenge their own and each other's behaviour.
- Group work between/with men/boys for the purpose of mutually challenging oppressive behaviour; and, for the purposes of strategic networking, to challenge structural forms of oppression. For instance, group work could be used to reinforce activities tackled in the two points raised above. Alternatively, group work between fathers at a family centre might be facilitated by a male worker who may, or may not, be a father himself. The focus of such group work might be how to parent one's children in such a way as to actively promote anti-oppressive attitudes and behaviour in them. Without concerted efforts in this direction, the entry of more men into child-rearing alone may simply replicate the inculcation of oppressive attitudes and behaviour in children, particularly boys – just because a father engages in more child-rearing, clearly does not guarantee that the model he presents to his child will be anti-oppressive. Quite the opposite may sometimes be the case.

- Creating positive and structural change in agencies, institutions, localities or communities. For instance, men working in an agency or institution can individually and collectively seek to have implemented effective harassment policies or recruitment policies which avoid discriminatory practices.
- Contributing to structural change strategies at a societal level. For instance, men engaged with childcare in formal settings could seek to organize regional or national initiatives designed to respond positively to the campaigns of the Zero Tolerance Trust (see also Pringle, 1995: 165–166).

The examples I have mentioned above are not meant to be definitive, simply illustrative. Wherever men are working with children and young people – for instance, schools, community projects, nurseries, family centres, health projects, social work settings and probation – these wider considerations must enter into their practice. Of course, I am not suggesting that each man can be fully active in working anti-oppressively in all the domains mentioned above. Nevertheless, whatever specific actions a man engages in directly, he should bear the wider context in mind and as far as possible network with men (and women) challenging oppressive gender relations in other domains of practice.

Conclusions

In this chapter, I have attempted to address what is becoming one of the most contested, and contentious, debates in social welfare, namely the place of men in childcare. What adds a further level of complexity to the debate about men in childcare is the transnational dimension which has entered into the debate. As has been seen, the European Network on Childcare is becoming a major influence in the debate. Its perspective on men in professional childcare, based on some continental and Nordic Family Support models of child welfare, seems to reflect a less intense focus on child protection (especially in relation to sexual abuse) than is the case in Britain (Pringle, 1997b and 1998). This throws up some interesting issues, as there is considerable cause to doubt whether levels of sexual abuse are actually lower in continental Europe than in the United Kingdom (Finkelhor, 1991; and Pringle, 1998).

In the summer of 1996, following a series of massive scandals about abuse in welfare settings, the British government established a national Children's Safeguards Review covering out-of-home placements including residential care, boarding schools and foster care (Community Care, 20–26 June 1996: 1). This initiative demonstrates very clearly the extensive concern in this country about the levels of child abuse in welfare settings. The Review reported in late 1997 (Utting, 1997). It did explicitly recognise the issue of gender, but failed to address the implications of this for practice. Nevertheless, it may be that the controversies about men in professional childcare which have developed in Britain, and which this chapter has outlined, will connect with the renewed anxiety of the government about what is happening in welfare settings. This may have further reverberations in the rest of Europe – especially as the New Labour administration, unlike its predecessor, clearly wishes to be meaningfully involved in the European Union.

If a policy debate about the role of men in professional childcare does gather further pace here and abroad, then the danger is that it may become polarized along the lines of 'Should we have more or fewer men in childcare work?'. My central contention here is that this is the wrong question. In this chapter I have tried to demonstrate that the real question is 'What strategies can we devise to involve men in childcare in ways that will also maximize the safety of children?'. In Britain this sort of realistic, informed and constructive debate is beginning to take shape, for instance in the field of family centre work (Catty, 1996). Let us hope it continues and extends to the rest of Europe.

I have argued that men's greater involvement in childcare activities does have a real and vital anti-oppressive potential, with possible benefits for children, women and men themselves. However, if such positive outcomes are to be achieved, men's practices in this field have to be grounded in a broad anti-oppressive framework which places issues of their power and violence centre-stage. I hope the discussion offered in this chapter has thrown up useful questions, even perhaps some useful answers, in thinking about how to achieve that urgent objective.

References

Baldwin, S. and Twigg, J. (1991), 'Women and community care – reflections on a debate'. In: M. McLean and D. Gৢᴜves (eds), *Women's Issues in Social Policy*. London: Routledge, 117–135.

Barker, R.W. (1994), *Lone Fathers and Masculinities*. Aldershot: Avebury.

Benedict, M.I., Zuravin, S., Brandt, D. and Abbey, H. (1994), 'Types and frequency of child maltreatment by family foster care providers in an urban population', *Child Abuse and Neglect*, *18*, 577–585.

Catty, J. (ed.) (1996), *Men in Family Centres?* Newcastle upon Tyne: Save the Children Fund.

Chandler, T. (1993), 'Working with fathers in a family centre', *Working With Men*, *4*, 11–13.

Dallos, R. and Mclaughlin, E. (eds) (1993), *Social Problems and the Family*. London: Sage Publications.

Daly, K.J. (1995), 'Reshaping fatherhood: finding the models'. In: W. Marsiglio (ed.), *Fatherhood*. Thousand Oaks, CA: Sage, 21–40.

DOH (1989), *Children Act 1989*. London: HMSO.

EC (1992), *Council Recommendation (92/241/EEC)*. Brussels: European Commission.

— (1994), *A Way forward for the Union: The White Paper on European Social Policy*. Brussels: European Commission.

EC Network on Childcare (1993), *Men as Carers*. Brussels: European Commission.

— (1996), *A Review of Services for Young Children in the European Union 1990–1995*. Brussels: European Commission.

Elliott, M. (ed.) (1993), *Female Sexual Abuse of Children: The Ultimate Taboo*. Harlow: Longman.

Fanshell, D. (1990), *Foster Children In Life Course Perspective*. New York: Columbia University Press.

Finkelhor, D. (1991), 'The scope of the problem'. In: K. Murray and D.A. Gough (eds), *Intervening in Child Sexual Abuse*. Edinburgh: Edinburgh University Press, 9–17.

—, Hotaling, G., Lewis, I.A. and Smith, C. (1990), 'Sexual abuse in a national survey of adult men and women: prevalence, characteristics and risk factors', *Child Abuse and Neglect*, *14*, 19–28.

—, Williams, L.M. and Burns, N. (1988), *Nursery Crimes: Sexual Abuse In Day Care*. Newbury Park CA: Sage Publications.

Golombok, S., Spencer, A. and Rutter, M. (1983), 'Children in lesbian and single parent households: psychosexual and psychiatric appraisal', *Journal of Child Psychology and Psychiatry*, 24, 551–572.

Graham, H. (1983), 'Caring: a labour of love'. In: J. Finch and D. Groves (eds), *A Labour of Love: Women, Work and Caring*. London: Routledge and Kegan Paul, 13–30.

— (1993), 'Social divisions in caring', *Women's Studies International Forum*, 16, 461–470.

Gray, S., Higgs, M. and Pringle, K. (1996), 'Services for people who have been sexually abused'. In: L. Mckie (ed.), *Researching Women's Health: Methods and Process*. Salisbury: Quay Books, 177–200.

— (1997), 'User-centred responses to child sexual abuse: the way forward?', *Child and Family Social Work*, 2, 49–57.

Grimwood, C. and Popplestone, R. (1993), *Women, Management and Care*. London: Macmillan.

Hallett, C. (1995), 'Child abuse: an academic overview'. In: P. Kingston and B. Penhale (eds), *Family Violence and the Caring Professions*. London: Macmillan, 23–49.

Hanks, H. and Saradjian, J. (1991), 'Women who abuse children sexually: characteristics of sexual abuse of children by women', *Human Systems: The Journal of Systemic Consultation and Management*, 2, 247–262.

Heward, C. (1996), 'Masculinities and families'. In: M. Mac an Ghaill (ed.), *Understanding Masculinities*. Buckingham: Open University Press, 35–49.

HMSO (1992), *Choosing With Care: The Report of the Committee of Inquiry into the Selection, Development, and Management of Staff in Children's Homes*. London: HMSO.

Holt, C. (1992), *Developing Effective Work with Men in Family Centres*. Mimeograph. Barnardos.

Hunt, P. (1994), *Report of the Independent Inquiry into Multiple Abuse in Nursery Classes in Newcastle upon Tyne*. Newcastle upon Tyne: City Council of Newcastle upon Tyne.

Jensen, J.J. (1996), *Men as Workers in Childcare Services*. Brussels: European Commission.

Kelly, L. (1996), 'When does the speaking profit us?: reflections on the challenges of developing feminist perspectives on abuse and violence by women'. In: M. Hester, L. Kelly and J. Radford (eds), Women, Violence and Male Power. Buckingham: Open University Press, 34–49.

—, Regan, L. and Burton, S. (1991), *An Exploratory Study of the Prevalence of Sexual Abuse in a Sample of 16–21-Year-Olds*. London: Polytechnic Of North London.

Margolin, L. (1991), 'Child sexual abuse by non-related care-givers', *Child Abuse and Neglect, 15*, 213–221.

— (1993), 'In their parent's absence: sexual abuse in childcare', *Violence Update*, May, 1–8.

Marsiglio, W. (1995), *Fatherhood: Contemporary Theory, Research and Social Policy*. Thousand Oaks CA: Sage.

Moss, P. (1994), 'Father, dear father', *Community Care*, Oct/Nov.

Nunno, M. and Rindfleisch, N. (1991), 'The abuse of children in out of home care', *Children and Society, 5*, 295–305.

Patterson, C.J. (1992), 'Children of lesbian and gay parents', *Child Development, 63*, 1025–1042.

Phillips, A. (1993), *The Trouble with Boys: Parenting the Men of the Future*. London: Pandora.

Pringle, K. (1990), *Managing to Survive*. Barkingside: Barnardos.

— (1992), 'Child sexual abuse perpetrated by welfare personnel and the problem of men', *Critical Social Policy, 36*, 4–19.

— (1993a), 'Gender issues in child sexual abuse committed by foster carers: a case study for the welfare services?'. In: Ferguson, H., Gilligan, R. and Torode, R. (eds), *Surviving Childhood Adversity*. Dublin: Social Studies Press, 245–256.

— (1995), *Men, Masculinities and Social Welfare*. London: UCL Press.

— (1997a), 'Men in childcare'. In: J. Popay, J. Hearn and J. Edwards (eds), *Men, Gender Divisions and Welfare*. London: Routledge.

— (1997b), 'Protecting children in England and Wales'. In: M. Harder and K. Pringle (eds), *Protecting Children in Europe: Towards a New Millennium*. Aalborg, Denmark: Aalborg University Press.

— (1997c, unpublished), 'Report on joint comparative fatherhood research project'. Universities of Gothenburg and Sunderland.

— (1998), *Children and Social Welfare: European Perspectives*. Buckingham: Open University Press

Rickford, F. (1992), 'Fostering with pride', *Social Work Today, 28*, May, 12–13.

Rosenthal, J.A., Motz, J.K., Edmonson, D.A. and Groze, V. (1991), 'A descriptive study of abuse and neglect in out-of-home placement', *Child Abuse and Neglect, 15*, 249–260.

Ruxton, S. (1991), '"What's he doing at the family centre?": the dilemmas of men who care for children.' MA dissertation, Polytechnic of North London.

Ryan, P., McFadden, E.J. and Wienceck, P. (1988), 'Case work services in preventing abuse in family foster care'. Paper presented at National Symposium on Child Victimization, Anaheim CA, United States.

Segal, L. (1990), *Slow Motion: Changing Masculinities, Changing Men*. London: Virago Press.

Thompson, N. (1995), 'Men and anti-sexism', *British Journal of Social Work*, 25, 459–475.

Utting, W. (1997), *People Like Us: Report of the review of the safeguards for children living away from home*. London: Department of Health and Welsh Office.

15 Child Protection, Risk and Allegations

Andy Bateman
Sheffield Chidren's Centre

Introduction

The title of this chapter could just as appropriately have been 'Coping with Abuse Issues'. We take it as read that child sexual abuse is gendered, perpetrated mostly by men, and that if this were not so then there would be no need to address these issues in the context of a conference about men working with young children. Our experience is that these issues are rarely addressed openly, but are constantly in the minds of workers, managers and parents whenever men work with children. This chapter will attempt to address these issues directly – by so doing, we can only enhance the valuable contribution male childcare workers are already making to children's lives all over Europe.

Recent events in Belgium have shown that child sexual abuse is not just a British issue, but one that affects other European cultures as well as all social backgrounds. Research in the UK and the United States shows that it is mainly, although not exclusively, perpetrated by men. Policy-makers and workers in the field have a responsibility to take this issue seriously – primarily for the protection and benefit of all our children, but also for the protection and benefit of those men who wish to work with them.

The initial focus of this chapter is risk. Risk is an evaluation which depends on adult judgement. As adults, we live our lives balancing risks and benefits against one another; and, as parents, carers and professionals, it is our responsibility to strike these balances for the benefit of the children in our care. The assessment of risk is a minute-to-minute activity that, as adults, we are usually scarcely aware of, but which we notice the moment a situation becomes complicated or controversial. However, when it comes to the issue of protecting children from abuse, the idea of risk assessment has become totally mystified. We choose generally to leave this issue to 'experts' who we ask to tell us what to do and we rarely talk to each other.

The field of childcare is no different in this respect from any other area of life. Over the last ten years the level of awareness and concern about child sexual abuse in society has expanded massively following the Cleveland investigation. Over those same ten years the number of kinds of childcare provision and the number of men working in those provisions has increased considerably. However, looking at provisions we believe that policies and practices have developed very little constructive reflection of the facts. These are that:

- male workers in childcare provisions will all be seen from time to time as threats to the children there;
- there is no doubt that at any given time some of those men are in fact a threat to children.

I make no apology for describing the situation in such bald terms – to do otherwise is to perpetuate what I believe is a collusion that hampers all of our efforts to protect children and promote the role of men in the care of children. This collusion is an unspoken assumption shared by both genders, that child protection and risk assessment are women's responsibilities, contributed to by men only with women's permission and approval. Women benefit from this collusion through enhanced power and men benefit through reduced responsibility. To give a concrete example of this collusion, at a recent training seminar, during a discussion about child sexual abuse, a woman participant said that 40 per cent of child abuse was perpetrated by women. Another woman interrupted to clarify that this was including all forms of abuse, and that 90 per cent of child sexual abuse was perpetrated by men. Male participants, workers with children, confided that they felt supported by the first woman and attacked by the second, who had merely exposed a fudge.

Men will not feel equal and work equally alongside their women colleagues to protect children while we all contrive to collude and fudge this issue.

This chapter will look at how the goal of men taking their place working equally with women to care for and protect children to the benefit of all can be reconciled with the gendered nature of abuse. It will consider how workers, managers and parents can together develop strategies as working practices and policies which safeguard primarily the children but ultimately everyone involved in childcare.

However, first let us look at some examples of the consequences of our present situation. A male worker from the Sheffield Children's Centre was temporarily allocated to another agency's children's service, at its request, to provide a positive role model for children and families using the service. A child was attending this provision who had previously been subjected to sexual abuse and was now in the process of adoption. The adoptive parents approached the managers and requested that this man refrain from any interaction with the child. They feared this child might exhibit sexualized behaviour towards the worker as she had been abused by a man. The manager directed the other staff (female) to interpose themselves between the worker and the child so that no interaction could occur. The worker himself was excluded from this decision. What is going on here? What are the beliefs and values informing this decision?

Clearly, a major priority for the manager is to work with parents and listen to and take seriously their concerns. None of us would quarrel with this – it is the responsibility of all of us to work with parents. However, requests from parents always have to be viewed objectively and in the light of a professional assessment of a child's needs. If we consider the consequences of this decision, we can make a judgement about it.

The immediate consequences of this decision were that through the behaviour of the female staff all the children and the parents were led to see the male worker as different, strange and potentially threatening. In the longer term, the male worker was withdrawn as the situation was too stressful for him to bear. Two major opportunities were lost – first, all the children lost the opportunity to experience a positive male role model; and, second, the abused child lost the opportunity to work out appropriate behavioural boundaries with a caring male adult. Anecdote suggests that the child, now a young adult, has not been helped by this decision.

It seems reasonable to suppose that the manager lacked confidence in the male worker's ability to carry out this important work, and to participate in open and professional decision making processes. He was treated as inadequate, and put in a position where he could not do his job. No manager could take similar decisions around a black or disabled worker, as such a stereotyped lack of faith would be contrary to written equal opportunities policies and the law. Yet this lack of faith was maintained in the face of strong supportive pressure from the Sheffield Children's Centre management, and in the end the male worker was made the problem by the other agency. Why is it that half of humanity is still regarded as a threat to children?

We believe the answer lies in as yet unchallenged assumptions about men's and women's sexuality, and about the two genders' different approaches to childcare. The assumption made in the previous example was clearly that the male worker would not be able to cope professionally with sexualized behaviour from a young girl. The child's adoptive mother had also said that she feared that the worker might abuse the child. Although I feel for the mother of an abused child, I believe that this fear is based in part on a common but rarely acknowledged belief that men cannot control their sexual urges and are biologically incapable of resisting any apparent sexual opportunity. This belief contributes to the assumption that 'all men are potential abusers'. It is a cry heard constantly from abusers 'I couldn't help it. She/he asked for it.' In our treatment of abusers, we rightly hold them responsible for their actions. A basic requirement for men working with children as equals with women is an assumption that men can manage their sexuality responsibly.

Following on from this is an assumption that men cannot protect children adequately, as they are the possessors of an attribute, male sexuality, that is seen as a major threat to children and which they cannot be trusted to control. Reflection will give access to much evidence that tends to support the notion that these two beliefs – that men's sexuality is uncontrollable and that men are unable to care for and protect children – are widespread in society. Existing gender roles support these ideas: plentiful research exists to show how boys are encouraged to be impulsive and expressive (less 'in control'), whereas girls are encouraged to be gentle, nurturing and unassertive (more 'in control').

The Sheffield Children's Centre believes that the act of employing men has to become an expression of two new assumptions – that men can take responsibility for their whole selves, including their sexuality, and that men can protect children. However, to accomplish this, men and women have to challenge many other old assumptions and take firm new positions. It is not enough to make warm and positive noises about how great those men are who choose to come into the work, we need to know what we believe are the risks and the benefits.

One widely held belief is that if more men work with young children, more young children will be abused. The argument is put that 90 per cent of institutional nursery abuse in the United States is committed by male workers who constitute only 10 per cent of the workforce – increase the proportion of male workers and there will be a massive increase in abuse. On the face of it, this is a powerful argument – it is a big risk to take. However, if we consider all the obstacles (prejudice, low pay, social isolation, stigma, etc.) in the way of men who wish to work with children, it is reasonable to assume that only very highly motivated men come into the work. These are likely to be of two sorts – men who have a deep desire to work with children and those who wish to gain access to them for purposes of abuse. It would follow that if we bring more men into the work they will be men less motivated at present to do the work. This group is less likely to include abusers, as research suggests that abusers are highly motivated individuals. Unless we believe that men learn to want to abuse through contact with children, increasing the number of men involved should proportionately decrease the amount of institutional abuse, and not necessarily increase the total, as all the abusers who want to gain access this way are likely to be on the inside already. A mothers' group at the Centre originated this argument.

The same group believes that a long-term consequence of involving more men in work with young children could be an overall decrease in abuse. We believe that a major contributor to the abuse process is the 'objectification' of the child by the abuser, the ability to ignore or re-interpret the child's behaviour and feelings. This ability is supported by a lack of identification with the child as a child. Boys who experience a positive role male model showing that men can care and empathize will be less likely to grow up into men who can objectify children to the extent that abuse is possible.

Research may help us to decide on which of these beliefs to act, but ultimately it is only through taking action that we can verify or falsify them. However, the Children's Centre has through its committed actions over the last 12 years gained some useful experience.

First, the Centre has learnt that the protection of workers and the protection of children is rarely contradictory and usually goes hand-in-hand. Over the years, the Centre has come under pressure from parents as the issue of child abuse has moved to the forefront of media attention and lost its previous taboo status. Parents have at various times expressed misgivings about men giving intimate care (nappy changing, toiletting children, etc.), and also put forward more general objections based on ideas of men taking away women's power by moving into the work. These objections have been met by establishing and publicizing a witnessing policy, whereby workers do not give intimate care alone but work together, and by pointing out to the parents that if gender equality is achieved it will be because each gender is willing to give up its areas of sole control. Some exceptions have been made in the area of intimate care for some parents, almost invariably for cultural or religious reasons. Interestingly, male workers have tended to advocate these exceptions and women to oppose them.

These decisions have not been made in isolation, but have been a response to on-going debate over years involving workers, parents and children. Policies and practices are reviewed on a regular basis to ensure that children retain their prime focus and that the rights of all are being upheld. The Centre has a Management Committee which meets regularly and includes parents who are child protection workers.

We believe it is no accident that the key to dealing with these issues is the agreement on policy. The involvement of men in work with young children is new and brings surprising issues into play. The training work we undertook with men working for other agencies revealed how little thought is given to anticipating what issues will arise from it – the anecdote given earlier is a case in point. The process of making polices which actively anticipate possible difficulties and issues arising from men's involvement in the work makes explicit, clear and challengeable previously implicit gender assumptions. These implicit assumptions unfailingly sabotage attempts to just bolt men on to existing all-female work settings. However, there is a reluctance on the part of both men and women to do this work, because it involves looking at and challenging those very assumptions in which they have invested their identities.

The issues that have been found to need projects in order to address them in policies and training are as follows.

- Men's confidence as safe and valuable childcare workers. We do not believe it is sufficient for men to derive their confidence as safe workers from the approval of women workers, as in such circumstances they cannot play an equal part. Some men have this confidence anyway, but others require the support of training to examine these issues with other men.
- Issues concerning touch and physical contact. These issues cannot be approached in a formulated way, but must be worked out with reference to each work environment.
- Issues of communication. As male workers often find themselves at or near the top of informal communications' 'pecking orders', they can easily be insensitive to difficulties of communication caused by perceived differences of status and power.
- The reality of institutional child abuse. Male workers often deal with abuse by denying it has any relevance for them, and then find it hard to deal professionally with their feelings because some work issues bring it home to them. If the reality can be brought home in a safe environment, more professional responses are the likely outcome.
- Child protection, the workers' place in the scheme of protecting children and their duty not to presume unquestioningly their

colleagues' safety, but to be alert to signs of potential abuse. It is interesting to note that the experience at the Centre is that male workers once alerted have very finely tuned antennae – this has emerged through their work supervising child contact visits of Schedule I offenders.

The real value of policy-making is that once made such policies act not just as a guide to action for all, but also as a contact between the workers and service users that can be utilized to ensure mutual support without leading to collusion that could endanger children.

However, even the best policies will not protect workers against false allegations. Although the Centre itself has not been subject to this, male workers in other projects have contacted us through the National Men in Childcare Support Network. Allegations in all cases have been found to be groundless, but not before the man's children have been subject to investigation through child protection procedures. One partnership has broken up as a result of this process. For men who choose to work with children, the stakes are high. Men can be made less vulnerable to an extent through policies of witnessing, open door, child protection, etc., especially if staff and parents are involved in agreeing them. However, not all projects are able to institute such policies in a way that involves and protects staff and children in full. It is clearly not acceptable to lessen men's vulnerability at the expense of children's safety.

In a nutshell, we believe that coping with abuse issues where men are workers requires the recognition and addressing of gender issues and stereotypes; the collective creation of acceptable policies to which all workers then adhere; specific training for male workers and all managers; and open communication between workers, management and service users. We also believe that this considerable effort will be more than repaid by benefits to children in the short, medium and long term, and that as men's input into the lives of children increases, this may well undermine the cultural processes that contribute to the genesis of child abuse.

PART 5

*Training and recruiting men to work in
services for young children: Are there
effective strategies for developing
a mixed-gender workforce?*

16 Are there Effective Strategies for Developing a Mixed-gender Workforce in Childcare?

Erik Hauglund
Royal Ministry of Children and Family Affairs, Oslo, Norway

I work as an adviser in The Royal Norwegian Ministry of Children and Family Affairs, Department of Family Policy and Childcare. This Ministry has adopted a plan for developing a mixed workforce. The plan is called 'Childcare – a place to work for both women and men'.

First, I should explain that in Norway, every preschool childcare centre has a preschool teacher as director, and each of the departments in the centre is led by a preschool teacher in charge of her or his assistant. Although, according to my dictionary, the word 'pedagogue' is a disparaging word in the UK, in Norway, it is the opposite, so I will use the Norwegian word 'pedagogue'!

From 1996, every preschool day care centre has had to work in line with a framework plan – or Curriculum – decided by the Parliament. This framework plan is a regulation under the Day Care Institution Act, and includes the following statement.

> Children need to associate with both men and women in day care institutions. As the great majority of children in due course are likely to attend day care, it is worrying from a gender-equality perspective that day care institutions seem set to remain a women's environment. A broad awareness of this is needed, both on the part of staff and the authorities.

As an adviser in the Ministry, I might have my own opinion of this particular task. However, first I will refer to the official plan for recruiting men and keeping them in the sector. I will then be able to express my own opinion later in the chapter.

I think Norway, so far, is the only country in the world that has devised a Ministry plan for increasing the employment of men in childcare. It is not a giant plan, and it is marked by having a female minister engaged with gender equality. By this, I mean that it is not the children's right to meet both men and women during their institutional childhoods which is in focus. It is more a concern about what will happen when most of the children only meet women during their childhood for maybe the first ten or 12 years – first in childcare, then in school and school-age childcare. What will be the effect of this in the long term, as regards gender equality? These circumstances are, of course, a source of anxiety. More than 80 per cent of children aged one to five years will have public day care, 100 per cent will have school from the age of six, and more than 40 per cent of the six- to ten-year-olds will have school-age childcare before and after school. During these years, most of the children will experience only women. The current staffing situation in Norway is shown in Table 16.1.

What are the main initiatives of the plan? The first thing to note is the formation of a group including one male preschool teacher from each of the 19 counties, contributing towards reaching the target of 20 per cent of the staff being men. This group was formed at a conference of more than 150 male preschool teachers. Those men are working with the principal government childcare consultants in the office of the regional commissioner, one employed in each county. Those two persons – the teacher and the consultant – are the basic group for planning and setting up initiatives in the regions. The plans they make will be sent to the Ministry, so that ministers know what is going on.

A group of men from childcare and education came up with a number of ideas they thought could help to increase the number of men. Members of the group included Tommie Nilsen, Lars Maanum and Svein Ole Satagøen. It is the background document for the Ministry's plan.

A video called 'Childcare, an interesting place to be – for men too' was sponsored. This video is used by our partners in the counties in secondary

Table 16.1 Number of men in childcare in Norway

	1991	1993	1995
Educationalists in charge (pedagogues) (heads of departments, directors of childcare centres)	411 (3.4%)	523 (3.8%)	687 (4.6%)
Assistants (not trained as pedagogues)	763 (4.0%)	1,015 (4.4%)	1,227 (5.0%)
Others (including specially trained pedagogues, caretakers and helpers)	1,270 (12.0%)	1,135 (11.0%)	1,532 (17.8%)
All staff			51,832
All children in childcare			220,000
Pedagogues in charge			15,044
Assistants			24,733
Others			8,609
In 1993 5.8% of all staff were men, in 1995, 6.7% were men.			

education, military services, in meetings of parents or of staff in local childcare centres, and so on, in order to try to recruit more men.

The plan points out that those involved in training preschool staff and local authorities have to make an effort to reach the targets. This is also mentioned in the minister's introduction to the plan. Therefore, one strategy is to challenge different constituencies to take part in the discussion of this issue.

Each year the Ministry will organize a conference. This year invitations will be issued to one female childcare director from each county together with male supporters and the principal government consultants to discuss three aims:

- how to get more men into childcare centres;
- how to keep the men there are on the staff;
- how to compensate for the fact that a centre has no men.

All participants at that conference will be practitioners, and hopefully they will compile a list that shows ideas and experiences that can be sent to every childcare centre in Norway. The strategy here is to point at the staff and ask, 'What can you do?'

This brings me to my next point. We must ask why it is that there are so few men in childcare? In Norway, the union says that it is purely because of the low pay. We know that this is wrong. It has to do with male culture and women's culture – boys growing up, learning that men do not work with children and girls growing up learning that women do. This is the vicious circle which must be broken – that is what it is about. That is not to say, though, that pay has nothing to do with it, but it is so much more complicated than that.

Some of the issues to be dealt with are not founded in research, rather they come from personal and professional experience. I would like to present them in some a somewhat provocative way:

- male culture and main culture (the press: aunts, napkins and snot);
- lack of knowledge of childcare as a place to work (men have never been there or, if they have, all they remember is the boredom);
- myths (paedophilia, gays, religious cults and so on);
- lack of consciousness in a female culture of the importance of men in childhood (understandable!);
- a female arena with female codes and ownership, created by women – for young men, it is rather scary to join;
- a non-existent arena for central and local employment services;
- low pay and bad prospects – they think.

As can be seen, these are all issues that can hardly be helped by government efforts or money alone. The Ministry is well aware of this – its plan is realistic to the core. The experiences so far are good. When you focus on a subject like this, much will happen just because of the focus.

The Family Policy and Childcare Department, dealing with family and gender equality, had the least men in the government administration (87 per cent women and 13 per cent men). I was asked to convene a group to change this, and one of the suggestions was to have a short-term goal of 20 per cent men in the first five years and a long-term goal of 40 per cent men in the next five years. Almost every woman, both in the group and in the department, said it was impossible. They believed that there were too few men with the necessary skill, men do not apply for these jobs, and so on. Today – one year later – we have 22 per cent males in the staff.

We found that more than 30 per cent of the applicants were men. When it came to interview, only 5 per cent were men. Could this have something to do with male and female attitudes, we asked. Women applicants who said they would like to work full-time in the Ministry, although they had young children, were treated like heroines. A man saying the same thing was immediately treated like a traitor – doing that to his family! Attitudes, attitudes and attitudes! Remember that these were the most experienced women in the country thinking like this.

Given this background, it is important to challenge the female culture and attitudes in childcare, which will be done at this year's conference. I have to emphasize that this does not mean that women do bad work. We know that almost every woman in childcare wants men as working partners, but we also know that this is commonly for a just one reason – they think that men will do some of the things they do not want to do, or at least take care of the 'wild bunch' on whom they already have given up. They do not in general think that having more men is important because of the children's developing attitudes and understanding and definition of their own gender. To understand one's own gender, a man ought to be as important for the girls as for the boys. Women's attitudes are not caused by unwillingness or stupidity, rather due to a lack of consciousness – it does not seems important at the time, and there are always more important things to do. Nevertheless, this is a matter of fundamental importance and women must cope with this by deciding what their contribution should be. Why is it that some female directors, working in the field for more than 20 years, have never had any problems with employing men?

Reading this, I know that some people will believe me to be a 'typical male', wanting women to do the job once again, helping the poor thing (the man), inside childcare this time, taking women's jobs and becoming directors or administrators, leaving the children to the women (which is one of the great myths of men in childcare).

What about the men? Do they need to do anything at all? Of course they do! They have to change nappies, they have to deal with snot, they have to wash the table and they have to do everything the women do. However, they must be allowed to do it their own way. Sometimes this is hard to accept for both sexes. Men should not be in childcare centres to change light bulbs or understand how to use the computer.

I once came across a situation where a car stopped and out climbed two parents with a small screaming face in a bundle. The smell of it told me what was going on. The mother was very anxious to change the nappy, but she could not find a suitable place. It had just been raining and the grass was wet. She decided to use the car seat, but the two older children in the car protested because of the smell. The father took the baby and placed him on the bonnet – all nice and warm after the drive!

Men and women act differently and both are adequate in their own way. They complement each other. So it has to be in life and work. Children should be allowed to see and experience this. Children not allowed to experience this will not learn that men can be loving and caring as a job. The circle will remain unbroken.

However, is a man's caring different to a woman's? So far we can speculate about this. In Oslo there is an experiment taking place in a childcare centre where all the staff in one department are men and they believe that there are some differences, but that that is not the important thing. Rather than there being some kind of a competition to prove whether men or women are the best carers (by doing the same thing in different ways), the common aim is to work out a better institution, not discovering the differences.

I believe that this is about ripples in water. When somebody focuses on a challenge, something happens. Currently, this is happening a great deal in Oslo and the ripples are spreading. The Ministry's plan is just one part of all this, but it is an important part – political focus is necessary to get the ripples to continue spreading. So far we are very content with what is happening. I will report back in 2001 to tell you if we have succeeded!

Conclusions

In 1970, there were two male preschool teachers and about five male assistants.

Twenty-five years later there are 687 male preschool teachers and 1,227 male assistants. In spite of no active planning from official authorities, the number of males has increased.

In 1995–1996, work began to further increase the number of men in childcare, and in 1997 a political plan was formulated to tell municipalities, educators and the public that this is an important task. It is too early to say whether this will have any effect, but of new students in preschool education for 1996–1997, 14 per cent are male.

Goal: In 2001 for 20 per cent of the staff to be men.

17 Training and Recruiting Men to Work in Services for Young Children: Is it Possible to Move Towards a More Mixed-Gender Workforce?

Leif Ærø
Viborg-Seminariet, Denmark

Introduction

What role do the educational institutions have to play with respect to recruitment and in their training programmes and study environment? These are the questions addressed in this chapter and which I attempt to answer. I also want to indicate some related research areas which, I believe, need to be considered.

Recruitment

The educational institutions are central in promoting the recruitment of men in childcare. If trained men are not available, then all the good intentions of municipalities, governments and unions to increase the numbers of male recruits are in vain.

In my view, the educational institutions hold one of the keys to breaking the unequal sex division in childcare. It is also in the institutions of education that you will find the potential to change attitudes and to challenge prejudices and myths about the position of men.

Unfortunately, we (in education) do not decide the wages, as a higher wage could provide the status necessary to attract more men. The institutions of education, however, do have other powers, as in the campaign to get more men in childcare, it is important that there is a neutral authority which is able to take the initiative and carry out aspects of the work, but which cannot be suspected of motives other than to promote action 'in the service of the good cause'. In this way, educational institutions are reliable and cooperative partners to public authorities and unions.

What can the educational institutions do?

They can argue the case for more men in services for young children from scientific, sociological and political gender points of view. I believe that we are succeeding in the European debate. We do not have the intense way of relating to equal rights as, for instance, in certain states of the United States. On the other hand, we are probably better known for seeking a compromise, discussing and negotiating, than for fighting in this debate.

In our work at Viborg-Seminariet we have never devalued the many years' work of female educators with the children in our institutions. We have stressed that we now know more about the subject, which is why we would like to put effort into getting both sexes working in the care of young children. (Men can always argue that they have a qualification which women do not have – they were once boys!)

The educational institutions hold the key to recruitment and they should work more actively with this role. Some of their activities are to:

- carry out research, as in the Thomas Coram Research Unit project or with experimental and developmental approaches;
- control information about choices in education and to maintain access to potential applicants;
- campaign on the issue;
- influence what to call the qualification in this area (in the context of the UK, show me the man who will be trained as a nursery nurse; the name of the training must be up-to-dated as it gives the wrong impression).

Research areas include:

- what really makes men want to do educational and social work;
- which training elements are important in educational and social work and which elements appeal to men in particular;

- which educator training programme will attract men.

It would be useful to draw up a list of what the qualifications in the different countries in Europe are called, maybe with a recommended translation list showing the comparable qualifications. Such a list would also be useful for inter-institutional cooperation.

What part do training plans and study environments play if they have to attract men?

In this section, I would like to raise some critical questions – questions one ought to ask educational institutions that train childcare graduates, if the education is to attract more men.

- Does your institution have a strategy on how to promote sex-equality among the students?
- What does your institution do to inform the tutors of the opportunities for men in education and social work?
- Does your institution have information materials about childcare education whose choice of text and illustration would appeal to men?
- Does your institution have short courses for men which introduce the area?
- Does your institution accentuate the special 'masculine occupation areas' of the education such as sport, Information Technology, music and outdoor-life?
- Does your institution emphasize particular areas within the curriculum which are more likely to attract men?
- What has your institution done in order to make your own study environment 'men friendly', for example good sports facilities, clubs or open creative workshops?
- Does your institution contain special study programmes which will attract men?
- What kinds of freedom do the male students have to influence your institution's environment?
- What are the initial reactions of men looking at your institution — would they want to be part of it?

I think it is worthwhile here to consider the importance of these questions by investigating:

- if it is correct that some of the subjects in this section especially attract men;
- whether the training programmes of institutions of education are up-to-date, in the sense that they work with a differentiated view of sex-socialization;
- which is the key idea in the project and whether it is of particular interest for men.

Are there any legislative conditions which discriminate against men gaining educational or social work qualifications? It might be interesting to see how the role of the ideal tutor would look if it included pointing out men's place in the childcare service.

The Viborg campaign

In 1994, the Viborg-Seminariet took the initiative for the campaign called 'Children Also Need Men'. We contacted the equality adviser at the employment agency and two of the largest unions for social educators in the County of Viborg. In Denmark, the union position is stronger than I understand it to be in other countries, and there is a democratic tradition of involving the unions at all levels of decision-making. Together, we formed a 'think tank' and developed a sequence of events for the work containing three elements.

The first element was an information campaign directed towards qualified men who were presumed not be motivated to be, or not thinking of becoming, social educators. Their attention had to be drawn to the values, possibilities and challenges contained in the social educator training programme.

The second element was the preparation of a report for lecturers in this area. The report, entitled 'When men want to be social educators', contributed to the comprehensive view of some of the problems arising when men look to join the educational profession. Furthermore, the report contained a catalogue of ideas for the training of these men.

The report became a best-seller. A great many students at educational institutions all over the country got, among other things, inspiration for their specialization project.

The report became a reality because a colleague and I at the Viborg-Seminariet received a small grant for research into the area. Among other things, we examined what kind of literature existed; and who was leading the research in the area in Denmark and conducted in-depth interviews with them.

Finally, we had the opportunity to take part in the first world conference for and about men in Stockholm in the spring of 1995.

The third element in the campaign was a 20-week pre-admission course for motivated men who only lacked qualifications for acceptance at the institutions of education. The course improved their chances of admission.

This course was carried out. In the written evaluation, in answering the question, 'Did this course contribute to you being clearer in relation to what you want to do in the future?', one participant replied, 'I am extremely clear. I want to work within the educational and social area. I want to make a difference!'

The whole project received a surprisingly high-profile coverage in national newspapers and on both Danish television channels. It was due, in part, to our appeal to the Danish Equal Opportunities Commission for permission to give men who finished the course satisfactorily positive, special treatment for their admission. 'Positive special treatment' is the 'open sesame' for access to the media in Denmark! However, the Commission turned down the application because it would not give positive, special treatment in an area where there were men already. The same would have been the case for women. The refusal, which arrived a few months later, caused the same press coverage – so that aspect of the campaign worked.

The entire effort means that we in Denmark have raised the proportion of men in the 32 institutions of education. During the last 10 years the figure has been about 17 per cent, but it has now reached between 20 and 30 per cent. A further consequence of the campaign was that educational institutions discussed the question of sex-equality percentages, and many ideas arose. One of the more effective was the idea of offering a sport option. Three institutions have already done that and it attracted quite a lot of men. These institutions reached 30 per cent of male applicants in the first year they offered a sport option.

As a colleague said to me, 'You can save your campaign and your theory. Offer something that directly appeals to young men, something with action, such as sport then they will come pouring in.' A female student said, 'Tell them how many beautiful women there are here, then they will come!'

About the course

On to the course we admitted 32 participants who all received financial support because they were unemployed. Of these, 18 completed, five dropped out (two got a job and three were asked to leave the course because of absences). Twelve participants applied for the Social Educator Training Programme and 11 were admitted. Two became teachers' assistants, two are about to qualify for admittance, one now has his own business, one is unemployed, and one became a night porter

· The course was judged to have been successful from the labour market perspective.

The course was organized in the following way.

Two weeks   Introduction

Seven weeks   Curriculum subjects (education studies/psychology, social studies, communication, organization and management, sport science subjects, out-door-life, music and drama, 'the man of the week' and 'the surprise of the week')

Four weeks   Practice

Four weeks   Project-work

Three weeks   Curriculum subjects

The evaluation

What were these men concerned about? Their own social interaction had a high priority. Professionally they were very interested in the education studies and psychology. They found it interesting to learn about themselves as part of the community – locally and nationally – as they had never seen themselves in that way before. Outdoor activities, video production, their own influence on democratic decision-making and becoming aware of themselves, group project work, the excursions, the dialogue, and the insights into the social educator programme – generally, they wanted more time for everything.

Making their mark
They confirmed that they were male students by arranging:

* the Christmas lunch for 300 students at the institute;
* presentations about themselves and why they were at the institute;
* two large-scale children's projects in the day care centre of the institute, including a Robin Hood project in and by a lake, which the staff as well as the parents still remember.

In summary
There is much to be said in favour of encouraging more men to work in services for young children. There seems to be broad agreement about the following, and the debates arising from them:

* children need male as well as female models during their childhood (this is for the sex-socialization debate);
* institutions and school environments are dominated by female standards (this is for the equal opportunities debate);
* workplaces for adults run better with mixed-sex workforces (this is for the working environment debate);
* teaching practice becomes more diversified if both sexes can mark their practice (this is for the socialization debate).

Why don't men come by themselves?
One could reasonably ask why so few men are attracted to educational and social work. Several enquiries in the Scandinavian countries show at least four factors, which we also found in the Viborg project:

- the salary is too small;
- the job has low status;
- the workplaces are too female dominated;
- tradition means that young men do not consider the possibilities of working in services for young children.

The salary
A former Norwegian banker – now a social educator – says, 'I do not understand why they paid me more for taking care of people's money than they pay me now for taking care of their children.'

The status
Job status and salary go hand-in-hand. High salary gives high status. However, many factors come into play when you evaluate the question from a status standpoint. A number of myths and generalizations frighten men away – perhaps also as a result of society's attitudes towards paedophilia, homosexuality and incest plus the industry concerning sex and pornography with children. Those are 'hot' topics which are connected with men: they are taboos, myths and generalizations. That's the way *men* are! More generalizations follow (we know them from the equal opportunities debate): 'men are greedy for power' or 'addicted to drinking and violent'. We face entrenched positions, myths and popular press images.

On the positive side, we find that men in education and social work are praised for being creative, flexible and open to new ideas – qualities which we welcome in education and social work. The way men 'grasp' the care is different to the way women do, and it is valued, not least by boys, but also by their parents. It is a myth that men can't give care. However, the care is not carried out in the same way that women carry it out.

The female dominance in the workplace
As about 80–90 per cent of the staff in education and social work in Denmark are women, and they have been for more than 100 years, it is obvious that they have organized their institution or school by female

standards and have created a female culture. Men in the metal work industries also create their own special environments. Many men find it difficult to identify themselves with the female-dominated culture and they find it difficult to live in. What do the male workers do? Some adjust themselves – unfortunately, not only for themselves but also for their female colleagues in the workplace. The women expect that the men will add something different, namely the masculine aspect. However, one man alone is not enough. The ideal must be a 50–50 sex division. Many men express feelings of isolation in these workplaces: they are bored, even though they find the work interesting. However, it is difficult for men to establish a supportive work community. An adult social life also develops during the break times, but not in a way that appeals to men. The talk is about the home, children and men. There is also intimate talk about their own well-being. The Danish research worker, Jan Kampman, is about to examine how professional behaviour with a group of children is conducted in a female-dominated world.

In Denmark it is obvious that many men – and much too soon – aim at leading positions and that they get them. Leading positions attract more men than women. Once again we are up against something sex-specific, and an equal-opportunities problem which belongs to the general presentation of the problem we are discussing. When we want more men in education and social work, we mean men working in everyday life among children, not as administrators.

Some men apply for union work and make a career in that area. In Norway and Sweden, several municipalities work actively to keep men working in education and social work. As an example, they are offered opportunities to create male support groups and to create networks where they can meet and discuss the work. The educational institutions also make use of these groups to recruit men for educational courses. This approach does not seem to be of any particular interest in Denmark. I have tried to make the union interested in such activities, but it doesn't seem to want to be involved. The Social Board in Denmark does not give priority to the subject. Maybe it is the local areas which have to work with the male groups.

Tradition

Tradition says that women care for and about children and that it is not masculine to work within education and social work. Women are 'nestbuilders', men are providers! Men are often met with suspicion when they apply for a job in childcare. There are examples of men being asked about their sexual orientation in employment interviews. Some men practice sharp self-censorship and restrict themselves in the work. Some easily exaggerate or misjudge the signals they catch from the surrounding world.

Conclusions

Training and recruiting

From talks with men training at the institution where I come from, I can say that the current education we offer, lasting three-and-a-half years, is very popular. The men are surprised about the range of possibilities within education. The study is problem-centred and organized around projects. The theoretical education includes six projects where the students are attached to a team of 40 students. The teams are offered a number of interdisciplinary lectures on a given topic. The team splits into eight groups (each of five students) and each is a base group during the project period. The group chooses its own topic within the framework. They have supervisors connected to their base group. The work is completed with a report. The creative studies give the possibility of choosing main themes and secondary themes. It is obvious that men particularly want to influence the choices during the training. We recommend letting do this. The projects provide optimum possibilities for this influence. It is also advisable to advertise this, to make plain that the content of the training is very different to that which most people would imagine.

Recruiting

At a conference in the Regional Public Employment Service in Århus (the second largest city in Denmark) the head of the region recommended that his region aim for 33 per cent men in childcare. The arguments are the same as we found in the equal opportunities debate in many other places. The public employment service in Viborg was also very cooperative about the recruitment of men – they stood financially behind our cause and campaign in Viborg.

Recruiting campaigns must be balanced. They must be serious and, among other things, must accentuate the masculine part of the job and, in the social and psychological elements of their training, highlight the very important task that they are carrying out. I say this in the light of our experiences with the campaign. Press coverage is essential if the message is to sent out, but it can be bad as well as good. The electronic media are particularly difficult to deal with – they are very sensation-seeking and they compose their own agenda. For the television media, you must have thoroughly prepared the message you want to get across. It must be brief (so brief that there is almost no message left at all) and you must be prepared to give it yourself or else they will gladly 'help' you!

A current concern is to work with maintaining the few men who, in spite of everything, are in the job, so they will not leave it or advance up the system. They are the best ambassadors we have. It demands a certain effort – and probably a higher salary – to prevent men applying for a promotion and moving away from the children.

18 Is it Possible to Get More Men to Train and Work in Services for Young Children and How Might This be Achieved?

Björn Flising

University of Gothenburg, Department of Education

Introduction

Unfortunately, if you look at the statistics for Sweden over the last ten to 15 years, they are not too encouraging as compared with the development in Denmark and Norway. In Sweden, there has been no increase in the proportion of men among the staff of day care centres and in preschool education.

As Erik Hauglund stated in Chapter 16, he was, in 1970, the first male preschool teacher in Norway. Sweden had its first male preschool teachers in the 1950s, but they were very few until the socially and politically turbulent decade of the 1970s. This decade saw the 'childcare revolution', especially in Sweden but also in the other Nordic countries. Young people and parents went out to demonstrate in the streets demanding good child-care and preschool education for all children. Government committees worked to form childcare services for the future and there were national and municipal efforts to increase the amount of childcare, with the aim that this should be a public service and a public good for everyone (but it was not until the early 1990s that we reached the goal that all who want to have access to a childcare service may receive it). During the 1970s, we developed educational theories and educational practice with the developing child in focus. Even today, these theories are more radical and progressive than the educational practice of the ordinary school. At the same time, there were lively discussions on equality between the sexes, including shared responsibility for child-rearing and childcare. We saw the 'new woman' developing her own skills and interests and going for a professional career and the 'new man', more emotional and caring, taking responsibility for his children and, why not, going into work with children or into other fields of care and human services (for example as a sociologist, psychologist or social worker).

In the 1970s, it was easy for a man to enjoy a sense of radicalism and progressiveness by going for training to work in childcare services and there was a substantial increase in the number of male applicants training to become preschool teachers.

As you might notice, I get somewhat nostalgic about this period. It was during this decade that Erik Hauglund, Jytte Juul Jensen and I formed our adult identities and we are probably still carrying some of the basic values from that time.

Then came the 1980s and the yuppie culture, the opposition to the generation of 1968 and the 1970s, or backlash you could say. We saw the rise of the materialistic man and woman, whose main effort was to earn their first £100,000 or at least enough money to buy a Ferrari or a Porche and a fashionable flat in the city centre. The role model was the 'financial puppy' (we called them in Sweden) working and dealing with money, stocks and shares or other profitable business. The percentage of men among those who trained for or worked in childcare services decreased, stabilizing at a level that we have had since then.

So, one of my answers to the question of whether it is possible to draw more men in to train for and work in childcare services, is that we have to reconstruct and recreate the guts and spirits of the 1970s in the Nordic countries. Of course, this is impossible. Society changes and we cannot reconstruct history. We have to work here and now and for the future.

Now we have the 1990s, the decade when the aftermath of the Second World War, the so called Cold War, has ended with the victory of the market economy. Today the message to Denmark, Finland and Sweden is that, 'If you don't lower your public finances and your costs for public services, such as childcare, you will not be accepted in the European Monetary Union.' The Nordic countries of Norway and Iceland have chosen to be spectators to this process, but the governments of Denmark,

Finland and Sweden shiver and try to adapt to the demands from Brussels (or Germany or wherever it comes from).

Sweden has, since 1990, raised the economic effectiveness of public childcare services by 30 per cent, which means there are 30 per cent more children in the services, but at the same cost level as 1990. This, to my way of thinking, means that there has been a decrease in quality, larger groups of children and fewer adults in the same premises.

To return to our question, 'How do we get more men to work in a setting that is under pressure of being perceived by the public as too expensive and too luxurious?'

Let me be a little more optimistic. Things are happening. On a Nordic project on these matters, I was the coordinator and Erik Hauglund, Jytte Juul Jensen and Johanna Lammi were the national representatives. This project was financed by the Nordic Council of Ministers and their committee on equal opportunities.

When we collected the statistics in 1992, we found that in Norway and Sweden men constituted 3.5–4 per cent of the staff in day care centres. In Finland it was close to 5 per cent and Iceland had under 1 per cent. Denmark was the deviant nation with about 10 per cent men among the staff of preschool services.

If we look at the figures concerning staff for older children, namely school-age childcare services, we might be more pleased. In Denmark 25 per cent, in Sweden 17 per cent and in Norway 12 per cent of these staff are men.

The aim of this Nordic project was to find good examples of measures taken to recruit more men to work in public childcare services. My first task, at the beginning of the project, was to make telephone calls to municipalities in Sweden and to ask them if they made any special efforts, or had any policy or programmes to recruit men to work in childcare services. This was 1991, the first year of heavy cuts in public expenditure in Sweden. The general answer to my question was 'We don't recruit at all; our problem is what to do with the staff already employed, so of course we don't have any special strategies to recruit men.' Later on, we sent out a questionnaire to municipalities and to universities and colleges for education for preschool teachers in Iceland, Norway and Sweden. The result was the same. Nearly everyone said that the issue of getting more men to work in public childcare was very important, but due to the state of public expenditure hardly anyone had any strategies to achieve this goal.

Anyhow, we collected some examples, had productive meetings in the project group and ended the project with a fairly large Nordic conference where we came to some conclusions (Jensen, 1996).

Information and 'marketing': encouraging men and adolescent boys to discover childcare services as a field of work that might suit them

There is a marked difference between women's and men's attitudes towards work with children. For girls and women it is seen as 'natural' to choose a job with children. Some might even say to them, 'If you don't find anything else to do you can always take a job with children.' This is not at all the case for boys and men. Childcare is not in that mainstream where boys and men construct and develop their work and life careers. Men often have prejudiced ideas about childcare.

Examples within this category are activities to inform boys in schools and young men in military service who are to make decisions about training for a profession or taking a job. Some video films have been produced for this purpose and, in some places, male childcare staff go out to explain about their job.

In Sundsvall, in the north-east of Sweden, they recently ended a three-year project aimed at changing attitudes concerning men in female-dominated areas of work. This was a joint project initiated by the munici-pality and the employment agency of that region. One main activity of the programme was to train 11 'ambassadors', men working in female-dominated professions such as childcare, school, health and social work. The main task of these 'ambassadors' was to visit schools to explain their work, but they also spoke at recreation centres and at some large conferences and exhibitions concerning working life, school and childcare, and other related topics. Within the project, video films, posters, pamphlets and other information materials were produced to support the work of these 'ambassadors'. However, the material may also be of use without this direct connection. Some of the 'ambassadors' also started male networks with men working in female-dominated areas of work. Another main aim of this project was to provide information on the gender aspects of work and to promote positive attitudes towards more male workers in public service jobs. This was accomplished by a series of lectures and study days for personnel at different levels of childcare, health, school and other public service work, administration and policy.

Due to factors mentioned earlier – rationalization, increased productivity and lowering of costs in public services – there was not a sudden increase in the men employed in these services, but they believe that there will be long-term effects of changing attitudes.

In Kalmar, on the south-east coast of Sweden, the university college offered an introductory week of preschool teacher education. The target groups were boys in their final year in school and unemployed men. For three days, 32 men had lessons and workshops concerning children and different types of preschool activities and for two days they had practice in childcare centres, in most cases supervised by male preschool teachers. This project was carried through in cooperation with the regional employment agency and local municipal authorities for school and childcare services. In conjunction with the introductory week they sent out information about work and studies in the field of childcare to 650 unemployed men and 3,000 boys in their final year of school. They had a work and planning group with teachers from the university college and male preschool teachers. They sent out a questionnaire to men working in childcare services and to male students in the preschool education programme at the university college and they organized a study day for these two groups. The questionnaire asked about male experiences of the conditions of work and studies in childcare services and preschool education. They received answers from only about 50 per cent of those who received the questionnaire. Most of the answers said that they were satisfied with the job and the studies. The job was perceived as interesting and important. The complaints concerned salary and status, and a tendency to get stuck in traditional gender roles within the staff group.

Try-the-job and on-the-job training

The project in Kalmar may be seen as an opportunity to sample education and training. In many towns and regions, the employment agencies offer unemployed men an opportunity to try a job in childcare on a short-term basis. The period is often prolonged as the man in question likes the job and fairly often he goes on to formal education and training for this job. This seems to have been the main road into childcare work for many of those men now working in childcare services.

Support, mentors, supervisors and networks

It is not the easiest task for a man to understand what is going among, or what is expected from, the workers in the female-dominated world of childcare centres. It has been shown to be a great benefit to have an experienced male worker to talk with and who can introduce the newcomer to how things work. This is especially beneficial during the practice periods of the staff training and education, but it also helps those who are trained but still new in their profession.

For a man, even if you have worked for a long time in childcare services, you may still feel isolated and in need of someone of your own gender with whom to share experiences. Male networks have been started here and there and the experiences are often very good. At least to begin with, they seem to meet a need for discussions on shared experiences. In some cases, the members of the network meet a couple of times and that seems to be enough. You know that you are not alone and you know others to contact either to discuss problems or to plan joint activities. Other networks may continue to meet, either regularly or occasionally, in some cases for years.

Earlier, it was not an unusual strategy, if there were some male childcare workers in a municipality, to spread them out as evenly as possible between different centres. The aim was to have at least one man in as many institutions as possible. Often these men felt isolated. Some quit their jobs and others tried to move to another institution where there was another man on the staff. Nowadays the common strategy is to have a number of men at the same institution, so they can support each other.

Analysis and development of the traditions and culture of childcare work and early childhood education

The care and education of young children has been developed by women. The culture and traditions of the work are transmitted from woman to woman. This female domination is not in itself a bad thing. On the contrary, it is probably one of the main reasons why the theories and educational methods of childcare and early childhood education are more humane and child-centred here than in school. However, it may be a difficult obstacle for a man to understand the situation and what's going on. One man said, 'You need to think like a woman to understand what's going on.' In Malmö, in the most southern part of Sweden, they have had a series of projects aimed at discussions of the day care and preschool culture and how men may find their place in it, or understand it well enough to take steps in order to form a male childcare-worker role.

It is important that women take responsibility for such an analysis among themselves. On the one hand, there is an analysis of gender factors in the formation of ideas and methods of work in public childcare services, of how women's culture and traditions influence the job and the organization of childcare and an investigation of the boundaries between the traditional ways women think about and handle matters of children, home and household. On the other hand, there is the professional educational work. Until they have completed this task, it may be hard to understand the roles of men and women in the job and to find the areas of work where they can meet in their profession to care for and educate the children.

Salaries, status and different strains of work

There are of course many other factors that may have an effect on men's lack of interest in work in the childcare sector. The salaries are comparatively low, the status of the job is not very high, it may be a noisy situation, messy and boring to tidy up, along with the heavy responsibility of looking after every child and the, sometimes difficult to handle, contacts with parents and so on. This is, of course, the same situation for both women and men and should not make any difference between the sexes. However, if you look for reasons why men don't show an interest in working in this sector, these factors may be pieces in the puzzle. Men might be more sensitive to such factors. If a man compares the salaries offered in childcare work with the salaries of most of his male friends, he usually finds the salaries of childcare work to be very low. If a woman makes the same comparison with her female friends, she often finds that her salary in childcare work is ordinary or even somewhat higher than most other women have.

I have not met any serious efforts to change any of these factors in order to suit men. Most people in this sector seem to agree that it has to be in the interests of both women and men to work for better conditions.

We like our job! We are not prejudiced about childcare or women's ways of organizing work!

A danger when you problematize a situation in order to find solutions for further development is that you might paint a very negative picture. In this case, it might appear that all men meet problems in their work, or that they don't feel satisfied or at ease in their jobs. In conclusion, I want to make it clear that the large majority of men working in the childcare sector say that they are satisfied and feel they are doing a great and important job.

The same thing goes for the problematization of men's opinions concerning children, childcare and women's ways of organizing their work. Many men say that they like to work with children, even young children, and that they do not have any problems in understanding women or in working together with women.

What I have said here should not be interpreted as if we need to convince lots of men that they should try the job. Instead, the task should be to find those men who might have an interest in working in this field, show them the routes in, help them to find the way when they get puzzled by unknown situations and to support them in the formation and development of their contributions to the important work of giving the children a good experience and developmental support. However, there is also a need to analyse the gender factors and their impact on the ideas and working methods of childcare. This analysis must be carried out by both female and male workers and is one of the main roads towards defining and developing the professional arena and towards achieving a more equal situation for women and men and for girls and boys.

References

Jensen, J.J. (1996), *Men as Workers in Childcare Services*. Brussels: European Commission Network on Childcare.

19 Men As Kindergarten Workers

Jari-Matti Vuorio
University of Helsinki, Finland

Introduction

In Finland, as in many other industrialized countries, places in the labour market are clearly divided between the two sexes – there are men-only occupations and women-only occupations. Only a few per cent of women and men work in sectors traditionally dominated by the opposite gender. Kindergarten teaching is one of the most segregated occupations in the labour force. The Finnish Kindergarten Teacher Union has 12,700 members, 4 per cent of whom are men, that is about 500 men. In Finland, kindergarten teaching is very well organized.

The first official kindergartens were established in 1890. Formal kindergarten teacher training began two years later. The conditions of admission for training as a kindergarten teacher were that applicants should be at least 18-years-old and should have successfully completed their education at a school for girls. Under these conditions, men could not even begin to think of becoming official kindergarten teachers, and I wonder if there were any men who were man enough to try. These preparation courses developed into more advanced kindergarten teacher courses which lasted for two years. There were no legal obstacles to men taking part in these advanced courses. In 1968, a new course was founded in Oulu. It was this course which first welcomed male students. The first male kindergarten teacher graduated from Oulu two years later in 1970.

In the 1970s special consideration was given to the gender of those individuals involved in preschool education. Public opinion favoured men as workers in services for young children. There were three reasons for this. First, the fact that an overwhelming majority of kindergarten teachers were female was considered to have a stereotyping influence on the children, for example making them think that all childcare work is typically female work. Second, the number of single-parent women was increasing and it was felt it was important for their children to have male models in their day care centres. Third, there was a general desire for the gender of workers in particular jobs to become better balanced.

At the beginning of the 1970s, a state education committee recommended that 25 per cent of student places for kindergarten teachers should be reserved for male students. The Ministry of Education decided that 10 per cent of all student places should be reserved for male students, provided that the applicants were otherwise qualified and competent. In 1973, experimental kindergarten teacher training started at a number of Finnish universities. These university training centres seemed to attract a few more men than traditional courses. Nevertheless, the 10 per cent quota was not achieved in any year. The kindergarten teaching profession did not seem to arouse much interest amongst men.

At the end of 1980, there was active debate on the quality and content of day care. It was determined that the kindergarten system better suited girls than boys. Boys did not enjoy themselves in kindergartens. They felt that their needs were not satisfied, their positions in the groups were not clear, their drive and freedom of action was not met with sympathy by teachers. Many boys were readily diagnosed as maladjusted, aggressive and too noisy. The teachers usually wanted to move these restless boys to special groups. Girls adapted well to the traditional day care system and they felt happy within the functional structures of kindergartens. The feminine atmosphere in kindergarten was regarded as a reason for the behavioural problems of boys. The educational culture was said to be old-maidish and no attempts were being made to cater for the needs of boys. In this public debate, demands were made for more men to be involved in kindergarten work. There was a strong belief that more men in kindergartens could solve these problems. There was a need for masculine role models and father figures who could make it possible for the boys to indulge in boy-type games, and who would understand what it means to be a boy. In spite of these arguments, however, there was no rush of male applicants for kindergarten teaching positions.

In 1987, the Equality Act for Women and Men came into force. Under this law, the quota for men in teacher education was abandoned. The share of men coming into the training of kindergarten varies from year to year and is now between 6 and 12 per cent. The share of men in early childhood service has stabilized at 4 per cent of kindergarten teachers. Estimates have been made of how many men leave kindergarten and change their occupations. Less than half of the male teachers change their occupations.

Choosing a career in kindergarten teaching

What motivates those who apply for training as kindergarten teachers? Choosing a profession is a process during which motives may change. The usual reason for choosing a career in teaching is that the applicant is interested in working with people and especially children, because the applicant finds their way of acting and thinking interesting. An applicant also finds a kindergarten teacher's work interesting. In interviews applicants say that they want to work in fields that are something to do with helping people and serving them. The practical aspects of the work are not considered at all. In interviews, women mentioned that working as kindergarten teachers would allow them be creative, that the job is varied and the work environment is interesting. Male applicants gave more weight to practical considerations in their answers; such as they could qualify in three years, the easy entrance requirement for the courses and that they believed that they could get jobs easily after completing their training.

Male applicants very seldom have had any vocation to become kindergarten teachers. One reason for this is that men do not usually know much about the practicalities of the profession. Men usually drift into this job, by pure chance, because they have had an opportunity to substitute kindergarten teaching for their ideal profession. There was a study in which kindergarten teachers were asked if they considered that men make adequate kindergarten teachers. Both male and female kindergarten teachers said that men were suited to the profession. In their estimation, male teachers were more positive. Guess why!

How to get more men to work with children

Last summer, the Minister of Education, Mr OlliPekka Heinonen, started a debate about quotas for men in teacher training again. He was worried about the fact that the balance of gender in the profession was affecting the educational climate in schools. To achieve a balance in the gender distribution, he proposed that men be given extra points for some criteria; that quotas for men be used; and that the admission criteria (selection policy) be changed. The information booklets of training centres should present courses in such a way that they do not present any jobs in a gender-stereotyped form. The Ministry of Education supports and develops careers teaching in schools and research into how professions are chosen. The Equality Ombudsman took a negative view of the proposals by the Ministry of Education, stating that any quotas in selecting students are against the conventions and laws of Finland. New ways to increase male involvement in kindergarten teaching are to be sought.

In a Finnish survey, male kindergarten teachers were asked how to attract more men to day care work. The best way to achieve this aim was thought to be to increase the salaries. One of the proposals was also to highlight the social importance of teachers' work. They suggested the incorporation of kindergarten teacher training with classteacher training. This aim was finally fulfilled in autumn 1995, when kindergarten teacher training courses became university-recognized.

How to develop selection

The trainers do not support quotas for men. The main reason for this is past experience. Too many men who came in via quotas have dropped out. Also, giving extra qualification points, for instance, for mathematics, was considered to be too one-sided. Good mathematics grades do not give any indication about an applicant's ability to be a teacher. The selection procedure consists of an examination based on a set literature. There are now proposals to change this examination to a more problem-based or data-processing system. Modifications of the subjects of demonstration lessons might be of advantage to men. When giving qualification points based on application documents, there could be areas of priority, such as orientation in social subjects, technology or hobbies involving science, sports or music.

Social position, image and the model occupation types are the main factors considered when choosing a vocation. Impressions of teachers and their work are still fresh in the memory when a young person is planning his or her future. Men are more aware of their career planning when making their vocational choice. What are teachers' expectations of their occupations, how can they advance in their careers? Kindergarten teacher training can now be undertaken as an academic degree (Bachelor of Education, 120 credit units and lasting three years). The degree obtained is in education, a branch of study which is not very highly rated. However, this new examination gives the students more flexibility in the labour market or if they want additional training. The degree course contains new subjects, such as early childhood mathematics and science. The basic work in kindergartens is changing rapidly, and it has already incorporated features usually associated with male traditions. When the general male population becomes more aware of what kindergarten teaching now involves, I think more men will come into the profession. Let us think positively.

20 The Sheffield Children's Centre's Experience of Recruiting and Training Men to Work in Services for Young Children

Chrissy Meleady
Sheffield Children's Centre

Introduction

This chapter sets out to profile the male dimension to equal opportunities work in children's services and to identify an agenda for change which acknowledges past neglect and promotes real equality of opportunity for male workers in the field of children's services.

Today, equal opportunities is a widely used expression, but it is not always widely understood. It is one of the most contested and contentious concepts ever to enter the child services debate. It is a concept that lends itself easily to different meanings depending ultimately on your political persuasion. You may come down on the side of equality of opportunity as 'fair procedures' or you may take one step further and say that regardless of procedures it has to be about fair outcomes. The parameters around discrimination have played their part in excluding male child-related workers from equality debates and programmes, and I would argue that there needs to be a recognition and acceptance of both institutional and individual discrimination against male workers in the field.

There need to be policies and programmes which seek to redress this imbalance and to ensure the outcome of providing employment that is fair and just. The National Men in Childcare Support Network at the Sheffield Children's Centre has advocated on behalf of men who have been subjected to discriminatory practices by employers. This treatment has been different and definitely disadvantageous and has been based on the myths and stereotypes of all male workers as only accessing child-related employment in order to abuse children and the accusation that men are trying to take over a previously female-dominated work area, which, as a result, has become a gender employment war zone.

This chapter will show how the Sheffield Children's Centre has endeavoured to include male workers within its equal opportunities framework and to advocate that a male dimension needs to be incorporated more widely in children's services for the benefit of children, families and male and female workers.

Recruiting male staff

The Sheffield Children's Centre has had an active policy of recruiting male workers since 1985 and in 1989 the organization adopted a policy of endeavouring to meet a quota of a 50 per cent male and 50 per cent female workforce. This policy was formulated by staff and parents with older children's participation. The rationale behind this decision was to:

- promote positive gender role models;
- challenge and break down gender stereotypes;
- promote gender equality in caring for children;
- provide alternative, positive gender interactions for children who had been abused by men;
- provide specific gender care for children from single-parent family backgrounds;
- reflect children's same gender care at home, that is lesbian and gay relationships/family backgrounds;
- promote equality of opportunity for all.

In order to comply with this policy, the Centre actively sought to make known its gender principles, policies and practices to the wider community through the circulation of literature in 12 different community languages, discussion at public meetings, seminars, training events and open days, by directly targeting men's groups, radio discussions and children's groups. Schools and training establishments were also informed, along with job centres and careers advisors.

Application of the policy

In order to apply the recruitment policy, the Centre ensured that job adverts were worded in such a way that they included men, again in a range of languages. Publicity was circulated to cultural and male centres, groups, leisure areas and social settings such as pubs, working men's clubs and sports clubs. The response was initially slow and staff and parents were delegated with the task of observing the response of men and women in particular male-dominated social settings.

In many of the large council housing estates in the city, the men's response was particularly positive and eventually eight men were recruited from these areas. It is important to note that, as a result of economic changes in Sheffield, the heavy industry base at the time was being decimated with widespread steelwork and mine closures which resulted in high levels of male unemployment. Gender roles were having to change as women were becoming the main earners mainly in the poorly paid service industries, whilst many men undertook a childcare role to support the family, particularly on some of the large housing estates.

In the more affluent areas, the response was poor and observers noted the incidence of peer pressure to conform to gender roles. Comments of 'ludicrous' and 'insulting to men' were heard often. Only four males were employed from these areas.

Of the total, ten of the men were from black and other minority ethnic communities and one was registered disabled.

As part of the recruitment process, positive action was taken to provide male mentors for the men which also reflected their social and cultural backgrounds. An induction programme was established which reflected the needs and interests of the men. This was formulated by talking to them directly and by gathering together research and information from past seminars, training sessions and discussions. The outcome was to ease male transition into the children's services settings and to promote male acceptance and confidence all around. It also served to break down preconceived ideas and, as a result, there are now 20 men in the Children's Centre who have a sense of their own value as men in the field of children's services. All the men recruited in the early period of the policy have maintained an involvement in children's services work and continue to be involved in the Centre.

Following the early recruitment, the Centre has found it easier to recruit men to its services and men have highlighted that the presence of other men was an attraction to the field and served to ease their concerns and sense of isolation. In relation to ethnicity, recruitment proved difficult initially, with particular cultures (i.e. the Somali, Arabic and Pakistani communities). During meetings with male elders of the Somali community, the elders expressed the view that men caring for children was against the laws of nature and gave an example of how lions do not care for their young. Male staff from the Sheffield Children's Centre responded to this with a description of Emperor Penguins. Following several meetings and awareness-raising sessions, a clear movement in perception became apparent and some Somali men were keen to pursue things further. The Centre organized childcare training sessions for them and practical work experience. As a consequence, they became Centre workers – both unit- and home-based. The home-based workers initially experienced difficulty with registration because of the rigid interpretation of language requirements. Pakistani male recruitment is now particularly successful at the Centre and headway is being made with Arabic communities, too.

The Centre believes in respecting individual cultures, religions and beliefs and this is an on-going area of debate in terms of men's roles. The Centre works internationally as well as on a local and national scale. It is actively involved in work with refugee children in areas such as Ethiopia, Kashmir, Pakistan, Palestine, Jordan and Rwanda. As a result of the gendered nature of the brutality of some areas of conflict, the Centre has learnt from experience that it is particularly important to recruit men to show an alternative and this has had proven benefits for all concerned.

Training

The Centre's expectation was that it would be easy for its male workers to access established child-related training courses. Appropriate training budgets were established to finance this and during staff appraisals, decisions were made by male workers to attend specific college-based training courses.

Differences in training establishment interviews became apparent from the beginning. For example, male workers were asked why they, as men, wanted to work with children and whether this was an appropriate career for them, whereas the women's gender was never mentioned or seen as an issue. This made the male workers feel uncomfortable – they felt defensive immediately and were placed in positions of having to justify their interest in the field from a gender perspective.

When accepted onto the courses, they were patronized or treated with suspicion or intrusive curiosity. This served to make this early training a negative experience for them. To counteract this, the male workers established a men only support group where they could discuss their concerns and support each other through those upsetting experiences.

At the same time, the Centre actively sought to increase the awareness of training providers and to encourage them to address the issue in their planning, policies and course delivery. It also advocated on behalf of men who were experiencing problems relating to gender. It was extremely difficult to ensure that the issues were taken seriously and acted on and endeavours were made to extend information and increase awareness. Since 1992 there has been a shift towards ensuring the positive recruitment of men on to child-related training in South Yorkshire as a result of the Centre's lobbying. Course content has also moved to include a male dimension, which has seen an increase in male interest and increased access for men.

The Centre has also aimed to support access into training by collaborating on visual aids to promote men into the childcare field. Additionally the Centre's male staff visit schools and colleges on a regular basis to talk to pupils about their work and to discuss social gender expectations and gender socialization. They also take part in 'Guess my Job' line ups in schools and colleges. To date, no-one has guessed their jobs.

Having established a group of male workers with a good understanding of the issues affecting men working with children, the Centre has found itself becoming a source of training, information and support for other organizations and individuals. This has involved the provision of specific training for groups of social workers examining gender-appropriate practice, child protection and the male role in residential care, work around sexuality and child abuse delivered to mixed groups of childcare workers at the request of gay and lesbian members of those groups, work on parenting skills with lone fathers and work on gender play.

More recently, a specific need has been uncovered for working with men in play, playcare and leisure provision. At a workshop at the National Men Working with Children Conference held on 29 June 1996 in Sheffield the issue of child protection as it effects men working with children was discussed. As a result of the contacts generated, it later emerged that a number of male play, play care and leisure workers were working in situations where difficult child protection issues were cutting across them and that there was a need for training that was gender specific to equip these workers to feel secure in their situations. In response to this Andy Bateman (a male trainer who is a parent user and a member of the Sheffield Children's Centre Management Committee) devised, in connection with the local Out of School Network, a course for male workers looking at child protection and child sexual abuse as they affect the practice of male workers. This course was positively evaluated and it is expected to be delivered in an adopted form to further groups of male workers including sports coaches.

In the process of designing this course, it was interesting to note that a considerable amount of work was needed to convince some of the women managers of the appropriateness of this provision. At an initial mixed session with workers and managers, it was clear that the women managers felt that there was a need amongst women managers managing male staff working closely with children to have specific training to help them deal with the child protection issues involved.

The Centre is also devising a range of other gender-specific training at the behest of groups and organizations both in Britain and further afield. The Centre is also a partner in Euroman and in Bristol's promotion of men into childcare, early years education and playwork as well as other initiatives. All training at the Centre for men has endeavoured to be child-centred as well as having the aim of supporting male workers in a range of ways and promoting their access into the predominantly female area of children's services. Currently, the children at the Centre are making a film for television about male carers in the home and in the Centre. They want to highlight their experiences and examine gender roles in caring for children. This will also be used as a source of training for all workers in the future.

Many of the men joined the organization with no qualifications or with qualifications from heavy industry. Male staff between them now hold the following qualifications:

- PGCE;
- DipSW;
- NNEB;
- BA Playwork;
- DipBE Playwork;
- Advanced Certificate in Playwork;
- NVQ Level 3 Childcare and Education;
- MA;
- PhD.

All staff attend outreach and unit-based in-service training and child protection training is delivered to all staff twice a year to update workers on relevant issues and to review their practice. In the Centre, training is seen as an essential equalizer and necessary for personal and organizational development. In the context of gender, it is seen as a prerequisite to ensure equality for under-represented groups in society, with men being one such group.

The Sheffield Children's Centre is committed to the promotion and application of equal opportunities and believes that children's services policies, planning and practices should incorporate a male dimension. Many public and private children's services have adopted equal opportunities policies over the last 15 years. Our brief examination of a range of equal opportunities policies in British children's services clearly demonstrates a significant variation in the range of groups covered by the policies, whilst some refer to gender, they clearly go on to clarify that they mean female, despite the under-representation of men in the field. A number of existing policies which do include men fail to appropriately monitor men in implementation programmes, whilst others later ignore men in recruitment initiatives and service delivery, for example lone fathers.

In summary, the development of equal opportunities policies in British children's services have generally not been consistent or corporate in approach and most policies in existence do not include men as part of the gender dimension of the policy.

The Children's Centre, in devising its equal opportunities programme, involved four basic stages:

- formulation;
- implementation;
- review;
- evaluation.

At each of those stages, a male dimension was included and the Centre has endeavoured to seriously address male workers and male and female service users needs and issues. At the same time it has endeavoured to promote protection for children and staff.

A commitment to equality of opportunity for male workers is essential if men are to be in a position to participate fully in children's services work. However, creating such equality of opportunity demands a recognition of past exclusion and an acknowledgement that male workers have largely had to fend for themselves (often unsupported and unprotected), a rethinking of existing policies and practices in children's services equalities work, and a trenchant commitment to making it a reality. In this respect, I have attempted to highlight how the Centre has tried to make this a reality and to indicate some of the avenues along which progress could be pursued most positively.

This is only one strategy, but the Centre feels that has proven effective and successful. I would stress that the avenue chosen – to promote equality of opportunity for male workers – should also have as a focus children and children's rights and protection, informing all practices. The area of recruitment and training is an evolving process at the Sheffield Children's Centre and is constantly under review.

21 Discussion

Kenny Spence
Greendykes Children's Centre, Edinburgh

Introduction

I have worked in a Children's Centre for the last 12 years. The number of people who were males in that environment has fluctuated between about five to seven direct care staff and six to eight ancillary staff (for example bus driver, caretakers and cooks). The first male worker started in a Children's Centre in 1981. The men work in a variety of locations in the 12 children's centres in Edinburgh.

As the number of men in comparison to women was so small – six to seven care staff out of a staff group of approximately 200 (about 3 per cent) – we decided in 1990 to start up a male support group for men working in this environment. We met together on a regular basis. The focus of these meetings was to:

- look at the support that the men working in an almost exclusively female environment needed from each other;
- share experiences of how it felt to be working in this environment;
- share experiences of setting up groups for fathers;
- share experiences of the effect men had on the children;
- discuss issues that had occurred because of the gender difference;
- look at how we would recruit more men into working with the under-fives.

We did find that one of the biggest hindrances to this was that the qualifications for a job in a children's centre was a nursery nurse qualification and the colleges only had one or two male students every year. Although the qualification has now changed to an SVQ in childcare, once qualified the individual either becomes a nursery nurse or a nursery officer. There is now a different qualification but the same title on qualifying.

The local authority also sees under-eights' childcare as an almost exclusively female domain and in its practice guidelines for working in a full-day group is in the section entitled 'Equality of Opportunity/Anti-Discriminatory Practice', which states:

> A decision was taken to deal with these issues throughout the document rather than have an identified section on them. Likewise, the discussion of when and how to use 'she' or 'he' concluded with a decision to use 'she' when referring to a member of staff and to use 'she' and 'he' in alternate sections when referring to the child.

This is despite the fact that there are male workers working with pre-school children in Edinburgh.

One of the difficulties we have encountered with regard to recruitment has been that, due to local government financial restraints, there has been very little if any recruitment. Fife Council have a policy that only internal applicants can apply in the first instance. Given a base line of no male workers for their under-fives, with only internal applicants, there is little opportunity to recruit.

In some ways, I feel that we need to change the language and the way we describe men who work in childcare. The Children's Act uses the term 'family support': 'Parents' entitlement to support are seen as the best ways to promote children welfare .... . Family support emphasizes building on family and community-based resources.' I feel that we should change the agenda and move it onto family support and the fact that all families need support and need people to provide that support.

I believe that the best way to provide that support is with a mixed-gender workforce. By focusing on the rights of children to have a gender balance among their carers, local authorities acknowledge these rights. They might then identify improvements in gender balance as a policy objective.

In my own personal experience, I feel that children benefit from both male and female carers. This is particularly important now that some children will not experience men as care-givers until they go to secondary school.

22 Discussion: Training and Recruiting Men to Work in Services for Young Children

Robin Wright
Lecturer in Childcare and Education, Bournemouth and Poole College of Further Education

Introduction

It is clear that, in contrast to the UK, the Nordic countries have implemented successful strategies for recruiting an increasing proportion of men into early childcare services. Effective strategies require three important steps (Jensen, 1996):

- a policy based on commitment, specific targets, objectives and priorities and a clear timescale;
- an action plan which sets targets, identifies means and resources to achieve these, delegates roles and responsibilities, and coordinates action and communication between the key institutions and organizations;
- evaluation/review which involves regular monitoring, assessment of the effectiveness of programmes and strategies, and development of further programmes.

The feminist notion of a 'critical mass' of 20 per cent appears to have been adopted by most of the Nordic countries, as being the initial target for male recruitment. However, critical mass *per se* is not a sufficient, if necessary, condition for achieving greater gender equality in childcare. Equally important are policies of political and economic commitment and support – at national and local/regional levels. Colleges and training centres also have a vital role to play. The Nordic countries provide good examples of this.

Since the early 1990s, Norway has adopted a national policy for the recruitment of men into childcare. An action plan aimed at recruiting and keeping men in early years childcare identified four key levels of responsibility – the state, the county, municipalities and institutions (see Chapter 16). Between 1991 and 1995, the number of male pedagogues/ trainers increased from 3.4 to 4.6 per cent; and the proportion of men to all staff rose from 5.8 to 6.7 per cent between 1993 and 1997. The target for 2001 is to reach the critical mass of 20 per cent of men in childcare. The Norwegian plan involves an on-going dialogue with regional centres about all aspects of policy. One of the points made in Chapter 16 was the importance of focusing on the issue(s) in question.

Strategies in Denmark have included an emphasis on the linking and cooperative role played by training centres. Centres also fulfil the important functions of engaging with equal opportunities, involving tutors and students in the process of communication about policies, providing short courses for men, examining aspects of the curriculum which may be particularly relevant to male care workers and trainers, and monitoring the reactions and responses of male workers and students. In 1994, Denmark mounted the Viborg project which involved 32 training centres and aimed to recruit more men into early years care with appropriate qualifications. The project included the provision of a 20-week course for older (20–40 years of age) unemployed men. By 1995 more than 20 per cent of all students enrolling on childcare courses were male – a substantial increase over the previous two years (Jensen, 1996; and see Chapter 17). At a recent conference in Arhus, the second largest city in Denmark, a target of 33 per cent of men in childcare in the region was recommended (see Chapter 17).

Both Finland and Sweden have implemented similar strategies to encourage more men into childcare. Finland has 6–12 per cent of male students in training and around 4 per cent as early years childcarers. Although the UK lags behind the Nordic countries in training, recruitment and employment of males in the childcare services, the Sheffield Children's Centre and Pen Green Centre at Northampton are encouraging examples of successful projects. Both have balanced teams of 50 per cent male and 50 per cent female carers.

A recurring theme in the Nordic countries is the need to focus on the specific features of male care – what men as gender subjects could bring to the care services. Related to this is the identification of curriculum areas which might be particularly relevant to 'the male experience'. To attract more men, childcare in general should be made more 'male friendly'. Perhaps changing titles such as 'nursery nursing' might be one way forward. Another issue was raising the status – economic and social – of childcare for both men and women, and not merely in order to attract men. Changing traditional perceptions of childcare as being 'women's work' is also important. Here the role of media has to be considered, along with all levels of marketing and publicity material.

Changing traditional/stereotypical perceptions also means engaging with traditional female cultures of childcare. Part of the struggle for re-definition involves identifying the social/sociological, psychological and cultural conditions through which gender separations and differences are produced and reproduced. Therefore, it is necessary to focus on those sites (family, school, work, media and religion) through which traditional gender relations, roles, representations and perceptions are constructed and lived out. Sites of the ideological production of traditional masculinities and femininities need to be seen in the context of wider economic, social and political relations. Discussions about gender are usefully informed by reference to sociological, psychological, psychoanalytical and culturalist accounts. Failure to do this, could lead to a treatment of symptoms rather than causes.

At another level, the language through which ideologies in particular and discourses in general are represented is important. Concepts/ constructs such as child, parent, father, mother, man, women and family, are used at times as if they were homogenous, somehow abstracted from the real conditions of the lives of real children, women and men. All such concepts and constructs are historically and culturally specific; what may be relevant to one historical moment may not be so to another and a strategy/ policy which is effective for one culture may not be successful elsewhere. Meanings do not always travel well across cultures. Historical and cultural forgetfulness may also lead to cultural and social imperialism with perceptions, assessments and prescriptions being formulated from an ethnocentric perspective which overlooks class, race and gender relations.

Different theoretical perspectives other than empiricist (e.g. ethnographic and phenomenological) have important insights to offer. Empiricism cannot account for the lived experience, emotional responses and feelings of individuals. The actual methodologies employed are also critical. Can one seriously read off cognitive and affective experience from visual responses to stimuli? Can verbal responses in one situation be taken as reliable indicators of actual behaviour(s) in others? Some theories (developed by men) may actually have underwritten female oppression, for example, sociological accounts by such theorists as Tiger and Fox (1972), Murdoch (1949) and Parsons and Bales (1955). Miller (1990a; 1990b) and Masson (1992) have demonstrated convincingly how aspects of Freud's theory (e.g. the drive perspective and Oedipus complex) have done considerable violence to women's perception of their experiences.

It may well be that in the struggle to change traditional masculinities and femininities, and to engage with existing structures and cultures, we need to develop a new language which makes notions of childhood, parent, man, woman, mother and father, highly problematic rather than taken for granted. One suggestion is to do away with the notion of child development and replace it with person development, in which we all play an active and reflective part.

Colleges and training centres have a key role to play in implementing the above. Some of the important concerns are to change negative perceptions of childcare and promote positive images; to adopt effective publicity and marketing strategies; to offer short courses; and to include course content which challenges traditional gender attitudes and ideologies of masculinity which may sanction violence to, and oppression of women and children. Specific points of action would include developing an ongoing dialogue with early years advisors; working with careers advisors and school liaison officers; and forging communication links with local media (press, television, radio). Action plans need to focus clearly and sharply on identifying target groups, targets for the proportion of male students and timescales. However, as Antonio Gramsci once put it, without sound theory, there is no effective practice (or strategy for that matter).

References

Jensen, J.J. (1996), *Men as Workers in Childcare Services. Report for the European Commission on Childcare*. Brussels: European Commission.

Masson, J. (1992), *The Assault on Truth*. London: Fontana.

Miller, A. (1990a), *Thou Shalt Not be Aware*. London: Pluto Press.

—, (1990b), *For Your Own Good*. London: Virago.

Murdoch, G.P. (1949), *Social Structure*. London: MacMillan.

Parsons, T. and Bales R.F. (1955), Family, *Socialization Interaction Process*. New York: Free Press.

Tiger, L. and Fox, R. (1972), *The Imperial Animal*. London: Secker & Warburg.

PART 6

Conclusions

23 Summary: Men as Workers in Services for Young Children

Helen Penn

Social Science Research Unit, Institute of Education, University of London

I have been asked to sum up, but instead of drawing everything together and giving a reasonable overview, I have been asked to give an unreasonable overview. This is not to devalue the excellent discussion which has taken place, but to try to view the proceedings through a different lens, to explore some gaps and see issues in a wider or different context. Given the time, this account will necessarily be partial and provocative, but I hope useful.

I have had a long and varied career working in services for young children. My career began unpropitiously as a three-year-old in a nursery. Much later, I became an infant teacher. I was radicalized by being a mother, and became a campaigner and, briefly, a local politician. I was an administrator of services, and now I have found a safe and comfortable harbour as a researcher. I thought it might prove a neat summary to present arguments in terms of each of these perspectives – as a child, mother, worker and so on.

My own experience of nursery was not encouraging. I attended a rather formal private nursery run by a Miss Daisy. I remember hiding under a big table in terror because I did not want to drink the milk at milk-time. I was terrified about the impossible task of explaining my dislike of milk to Miss Daisy. I knew that she would give me short shrift about the milk or any other matter on which I might have disagreed with her. After three successive days of crouching under the table, I was sent home – classed as ineducable – to my disgraced mother. I do not think it would have made any difference if Miss Daisy were a man, the milk would still have tasted disgusting.

If I can recollect the experience after nearly 50 years, how vivid it must have been at the time. My point is that we know very little about what children in nurseries think or what they feel deeply about. My hunch would be that they take their surroundings as given, as part of the way the world is, and they must come to terms with it in whatever way they can – the space in which they move, what they can eat, what there is to do, their friends, how the adults treat them, how far away the toilets are. There are many things going on in a nursery. Can we really single out the masculinity and femininity of the workers as the pivotal or even as significant experiences for children? Male workers here have claimed that it does make a significant difference to them although Charlie Lewis has argued – from a rather different psychological perspective, looking at children as objects rather than listening to them as subjects – that in domestic circumstances, the presence or absence of men, *per se*, does not make an observable difference. Certainly from a child's perspective, we do not really know about the effects of men in a nursery, and our investigations and methodologies are only just beginning.

As a mother, the first nursery I used was at the University of Canterbury. The mothers were without exception middle-class, and the workers were without exception working-class women and in awe of academic qualifications. The workers not only deferred to the parents, they treated them almost as superior beings. In the UK the profile of day care users is that they are overwhelmingly middle-class professionals, those who can afford to buy childcare, whereas the workers are overwhelmingly drawn from low-income households. Welfare nurseries or family centres on the other hand cater for very deprived families, and the roles are reversed – the staff are there to guide and counsel the poor and non-coping parents. How do we insert or reconcile gender issues with these powerful issues of class and status?

As a mother, too, what confronted me was an appalling lack of choice. My experiences as a mother led to my becoming, for a short while, a local politician – I have to say as unregenerated 'Old Labour'. From a policy or political perspective (and in some languages these are not differentiated – I do not know about Nordic languages in this respect), the major concern is the paucity and inequality of services for young children. We have heard that 80 per cent of children aged one to five are in publicly funded day care in Norway. In the UK, the comparable figure is 1 per cent. The political priority in the UK must be to establish more equitable, accessible and coherent services. In that context, men in childcare is likely to be the icing on the cake – it cannot matter to parents very much whether or not men work in childcare if there is no childcare. Moreover, the inequity of children's life chances in the UK is overwhelming – an estimated one in four children under the age of five living in poverty. If this is the case, again, arguing for men to work in childcare is not likely to have any direct influence on the circumstances in which so many children grow up. The overarching issue in the lives of children is the level of poverty of households and communities in which they live rather than the presence or absence of men.

From the point of view of being a worker, instead of drawing on my own experiences, which in common with almost everyone else working in early childhood services have been an experience of hierarchy, I want to draw from the study Susan McQuail and I carried out for the DfEE on childcare as a gendered occupation. We talked to nursery nurses (men and women) in training. We also interviewed their tutors and the providers of services where they did their placements, about their perceptions of gender and career. Our findings had much in common with the work described by Claire Cameron, Peter Moss and Charlie Owen. I want to highlight one small aspect, what I might call feminist backlash. Some of the women we interviewed were very irritated by the attention given to men, and the way in which men were seen to be preening themselves for coming into a female environment. They saw it as a masculine self-congratulation which did not arise from achievement or thoughtful change, but merely from a sense of being a man and continuing to be one in a feminine environment. Three quotations might give a sense of this tension. The first is from a male student.

Us being blokes, it's easier to get a job. Schools like males, the children need a male to look up to, the majority are crying out for males. But if it's like that then you can pick and choose the job you want, send out your CVs.

The next quotation is from a tutor who thought the men on her courses were problematic.

The men are spoilt and privileged, they get looked after by the women, and get away with a lot. The women are so pleased to have them. We are a long way from equity of treatment. It can stop them from growing (i.e. emotionally).

The third quotation is from a female student speaking to a young man (the only one) in her class, who described himself as 'a natural' and able to get on with children without any problems. Many of the women laughed at his claim, and the woman was clearly expressing a view with which most of the other students in the group strongly agreed, when she said, 'You're not harassed because we're tolerant. Women accept that men can exist in the world ... we have spoilt and pampered you, made your day.'

As Williamson (1995) claims, men do not necessarily modify their views on coming into a woman's profession; they bring their masculinity and male assumptions with them. For some of our sample this self-congratulation and failure to change or adapt was a source of indignation. I must admit to slight reactions of this kind at some of the discussion which has taken place.

Let me shift perspective yet again, to that of research. As a researcher, what has preoccupied me is how do you find out 'the truth'. What is it? Doing research in the social sciences seems to me less a matter of fact finding, and more a matter of philosophical or even political enquiry. What you decide to examine, the methodologies on which you draw, the way in which you talk and write about the work you have undertaken, are all contentious. We have had a researcher, Charlie Lewis, discuss meta-analysis of 200 mainly empirical US studies on fatherhood, and a response from Andy, a practitioner, whose own lived experiences have led him to very different conclusions. However, research is not definitive, no more than practice – they are all parts of the jigsaw. Just as researchers need to understand the grind – or not in the case of the Norwegians – of daily practice, so practitioners need to be rigorous and systematic in accounting for and describing their practice. I prefer to think of research as a continuum from lived experience to epidemiological distance, in which we can all play a part. However, here I think I am talking to the converted.

I would like to add one final category to my list of perspectives, that of traveller. For the last two years I have spent a lot of time in the developing (or majority) world, working for the Save the Children Fund. My experience in working for many different communities has been that childhood and children are not the same everywhere, far from it. A child is a social construct – I have almost come to the conclusion that there is no such thing as child development, but that is another story – and in constructing systems of care or education or health for children we have to take keen account of cultural diversities. The same goes for men and women. Being a man and being a woman in the majority of the world's population is not the same as being a man in the tiny minority of the world from which we have derived most of our information and examples, namely the minority world of the UK, the United States and the Nordic countries. I think we need to think very carefully about our assumptions of 'masculinity' and 'femininity' because, rather like notions of family and kinship, they shift remarkably depending on where you come from in the world. Male masseurs and female warriors are both human possibilities. These are extreme examples, but failure to consider the implications of cultural diversity has been perhaps the biggest gap in our discussions here.

I want to conclude by putting forward a different framework for looking at men and women as carers in early childhood services. I think we need to reconsider the paradigm we use for relationships between adults and children in early childhood services. We draw implicitly on the heterosexual model of the family, a mother and father bringing up their children. Suppose instead we try to conceptualize the nature of intergenerational relationships in terms of friendships. Some of you may know the work of Judy Dunn (1993) in which she describes friendship between children. She has suggested that the nature of friendship – its continuity and reciprocity – is a transforming experience.

> Friends can create a world of great involvement and high adventure ... they must coordinate their efforts with all the virtuosity of an accomplished jazz quartet and they must manage the amount of conflict between them. This requires enormous social skill. (Dunn, 1993: 109)

Friendship, she suggests may not only be a feature of child–child relationships, but a paradigm for adult–child relationships. We could think of children and staff in their interactions in nurseries creating the joys of friendship – affection, enjoyment, caring and support, making an exciting and distinctive daily world.

To do this, as our Nordic contributors have pointed out, is to emphasize the positive rather than the negative, to invert the 'risk discourse' which plagues welfare provision in the UK and the United States, and to put it in a meaningful perspective. Let me give you an example from a Spanish nursery in a working-class district of Barcelona.

> In this nursery the pleasure the staff take in one another's company, and in the children, is palpable. There seems to be an implicit view amongst most staff that of all the places in which one could choose to spend one's time this is it. There is a kind of joie de vivre which expresses itself not only in the staff spending much more time in the nursery than they are contracted to do, staying on to help on each others shifts, but with much physical affection and laughter. I watch a young member of staff and the older cleaner stroll up and down the courtyard, their arms around one another, deep in conversation. One member of staff in particular gives enthusiastic kisses to every child on arrival, and to some of the parents and their accompanying children, as well as to other staff. ('Handsome,' she says to a young boy and gives him a wet kiss. Then kisses his older sister who is on her way to school. 'You please me,' she says to another child as she bestows a kiss.)

As an English observer for whom such physical expression of mood is unusual, I worry about her extravagant kissing, but no-one else seemed to consider it intrusive. The children cluster around her like chickens round a mother hen, such is her warmth and glow. For instance, Marco, involved in a game with cars at the other end of the room, points to the traffic queue he has made line up at the lights; she shouted her delighted approval from the other end of the room and he runs to her for a kiss, before going back to his traffic control post. Two children come into the room crying. The member of staff sits them down to talk about it, makes soothing remarks, and then kisses one of the children on the back of the neck and tells him to be careful. He squirms with pleasure.

Although this particular member of staff is extravagant with her kisses, almost everyone shows physical affection uninhibitedly. A toddler strays into the kitchen, the cook picks him up, kisses him and passes him outside, where he is passed around amongst several staff and children, all of whom also kiss him. The children often solve arguments and seal their peace with hugs and kisses, boys as well as girls, sometimes at the direction of the staff, sometimes spontaneously. (Penn, 1997)

One could regard the physical expression in this nursery as pathologically dangerous for children. The young man in charge of the babies for example was uninhibitedly gay. He also caressed the babies he cared for with great gentleness and played them Bach harpsichord music to soothe them. However, I know from the many discussions I held in the nursery, and with city administrators, there was only a discourse of affection and friendship, and none of masculinity, femininity or risk. What are we to make of this? I suggest the example of this nursery poses questions we have yet to answer or even to address.

References

Dunn, J. (1993), *Young Children's Close Relationships: Beyond Attachment.* London: Sage.

Penn, H. (1997), *Comparing Nurseries.* London: Paul Chapman.

Williams, C. (ed.) (1995), *Still a Man's World: Men Who Do 'Women's Work'.* Berkeley: University of California Press.